ALL TIME FAVORITE RECIPES

ALL TIME FAVORITE
RECIPES

From Family and Friends

Compiled by Judith Braun Whitmore

For my children Carrie and Steven
with love, Mom

Judy's Grandmothers:
Miriam Grubman (left) and
Blanche Fielder (right)

My father's mother spent every Friday in her tiny kitchen, up to her elbows in flour. Literally. From her two small ovens, she could produce enough baked goods for a small army. At the end of the day, she'd lovingly wrap care packages for each of her three sons and their families—cookies, egg bread (challah), onion rolls, crackers, and apple cakes. Everyone in the family looked forward to Friday and Grandma Miriam's treats.

My first cooking lesson took place in her kitchen. I was nineteen and she was around eighty. We didn't really know how old she was because she had no birth certificate. She did everything by "feel." None of her recipes were written down. Fearing they would be lost, I decided to spend the day baking with her. I arrived at 8:00 a.m. armed with a pencil and a pad of paper. We began by shelling fresh walnuts for her Mandel bread. Packaged walnuts were not only a luxury for someone who had survived the Great Depression, she also claimed they had less flavor.

I did my best to estimate the amount of ingredients she used. For instance, she'd say, "a half cup of oil," then fill a clean drinking glass sort of half full of oil before adding it to the Mandel bread dough. She never used a measuring cup. A half spoonful of salt or a whole spoon of vanilla meant, *Look in the drawer, find a spoon that looks close enough to the amount you might need, and use that one.* Her challah recipe is outstanding. Even if you have never baked a loaf of bread before, I urge you to try it. It's not difficult, and it's fantastic.

My other grandmother, Blanche, was a great cook, and she wrote everything down. Whenever she invited her grandchildren over for dinner, she would ask them what they wanted her to prepare. For me, it was always her "Crisp Chicken." To this day, it's one of my favorite recipes. Her noodle kugel is the best I've ever had. Grandma Blanche's recipes tend to be short, fast, and easy. She liked good food, but didn't want to waste time in the kitchen. She had better things to do. When she was eighty years old, she was still taking her daily five-mile walk in high-heeled shoes!

Many times over the years, I've asked family members and friends, "Can I get that recipe?" Thanks to their generosity, my recipe collection is enormous. Some of the recipes have been handed down from great-grandmothers while others are most likely from cookbooks long forgotten. In any event, these are the dishes I was raised on and the ones I prepared for my children. They are my favorites. I hope you like them too.

-Judy

TABLE OF CONTENTS

Judy's Grandmothers:
Miriam Grubman (left) and
Blanche Fielder (right)

This book is

dedicated to

my family

and friends.

Bon
Appetite!

My mother, Arlene Grubman, and me.

Many of the recipes in this book are from Mom. Mom was a great hostess and loved entertaining family and friends. There was always an extra place at our dinner table for whoever showed up.

INTRODUCTION

About Judy

My parents named me Judy after Judy Garland. I was blessed with a mother who believed exposure to the great musicals of the 1940s and 1950s was as important as learning your ABCs. She would often rush into my room and say something like, "Your algebra can wait, *Singing in the Rain* is on TV." Her attitude was no doubt prejudiced by her father's position as a violinist in the MGM Studio Orchestra. Whenever you see *The Wizard of Oz* or *Meet Me in St. Louis,* and you hear those amazing violins—one of them was Grandpa. Skipping homework to watch movies was sort of like spending time with him. Grandma was also a musician. At thirteen, she supported herself as a pianist in silent movie theaters.

In the hope of growing the family's musical tree, Mom enrolled me in singing and dancing lessons early on. With my pre-adolescent imitations of Ginger Rogers, Doris Day, and Carmen Miranda, I "shuffled off to Buffalo" for my parents' friends, our Japanese gardener who spoke no English, and lost travelers who knocked on the door of our then rural San Fernando Valley home seeking directions. I practiced the piano every day because my mother said it would make me popular.

My immersion into the world of Cole Porter, Johnny Mercer, and Rodgers and Hammerstein led to an unusual anxiety. I spent my childhood waiting for a hidden orchestra to materialize at Riverside Drive Elementary School, tormented by the thought: How would my classmates know the dance steps when that happened?

During college I got a gig singing background vocals for Capitol Records, and appeared on stage with a local band in Berkeley, California. I also played Frau Schrader in a production of *The Sound of Music.* I pursued the "performer" path, while harboring an equally desirous goal. If anyone asked me what I wanted to be when I grew up, the answer was always the same. "I want to be a bride."

And why not? My mother's life was glamorous—a house with a swimming pool, a charge card at Saks, and a weekly afternoon card game where she and her friends ate coffee cake and smoked cigarettes. Dad loved seeing her enjoy herself. She was the love of his life.

Dad's family came from Russia, no Poland. I mean Russia, no Poland. The border kept changing, so they had to learn a lot of different languages. When I was fifteen, my folks wouldn't let me go to Palm Springs for Easter break, but when my grandmother was fifteen, she kissed her

Me and my father, Seymour Grubman.

I love this photo of me and my dad.
Dad always manned the barbecue
(and the bar) at our regular Sunday
evening dinners.

parents goodbye and walked across Europe by herself from Russia to Amsterdam. She arrived in New York, found work in a sweatshop, and eventually earned enough to bring her eight brothers and sisters, her parents, and her own grandparents to America. Whenever I have to do something really difficult, I remember I have her genes.

My Dad and Mom met when they were both in the Army. Yes, that's right. I am the only person I know whose mother served in the Army during World War II. On my piano is a photo of a woman in uniform. It looks like a head shot of Rita Hayworth. It's not. Dad thought Mom was a knockout. She was. When my father was wounded during WW II, Douglas MacArthur came to his bedside to personally award him two Silver Stars and a Bronze Star along with a Purple Heart. Dad taught me to be relentless when setting goals for myself, and his life and deeds speak volumes about the value of hard work, perseverance, and loyalty. To this day, my heart belongs to him.

I held out for someone just like Dad, adopting Snow White's mantra—"Someday My Prince Will Come." He finally showed up in the form of a fine young man from Beverly Hills. We married, had two children, and promptly gave up the family castle for a mountaintop home in Aspen. I learned to ski, can peaches, and saddle a horse. Our closest neighbors were the singer John Denver and his wife Annie. I cherish the memory of a camping trip we all took with our children. Instead of an alarm clock, I was awakened to John sitting outside our tent, strumming his guitar and singing *Rocky Mountain High*.

I served as the president of American Theatre Company in Aspen for six years. During that time we presented Julie Harris in *The Belle of Amherst*, Hal Holbrook in *Mark Twain Tonight*, Vincent Price as *Oscar Wilde*, and numerous other wandering minstrels. We produced our own shows in the summertime, among them *Barefoot in the Park*, *The Voice of the Turtle*, *The Tavern*, and *Mass Appeal* with John Travolta and Charles Durning. During the same period, I was president of the Aspen Playwright's Conference. We premiered fifteen American plays, including A.R. Gurney's *The Golden Age*, and Mark Medoff's *The Majestic Kid*.

My parents collected antique dishes. At formal dinners, Mom loved serving a fish course on these Limoges flamingo plates.

When I had had my fill of pulling porcupine quills from my dogs' noses, I returned to Los Angeles where I undertook my first independent theater endeavor, producing *Taking a Chance on Love*. With a rave review from Variety, I headed to London. I bought a house in Chelsea and co-produced Leonard Bernstein's *Wonderful Town*. About that time, my second prince (this time it would be "happily ever after") came along and I settled down in Pacific Palisades, California.

After having enough therapy to undoubtedly pay for my therapist's swimming pool and her Mercedes, I decided I liked the process. I went back to college and earned my Master's in Clinical Psychology. I gave up my West Los Angeles practice in 2001 when I moved to Newport Beach and became a writer. My first novel, *Come Fly with Me*, published in 2013, became an Amazon Kindle bestseller. Since 2003, I satisfy my thirst for the theater by working each summer as a make-up artist at the Laguna Beach *Pageant of the Masters*. I have recently returned to my first love, singing, and have performed in several concerts.

I am passionate about Beethoven's Ninth, New York theater, and the Lincoln and Jefferson Memorials in Washington. I cry every time I visit. I adore thin-crust pizza, In 'n Out Burgers, and pasta with truffles. I'm in awe of my sister and brother, who have devoted twenty-five years to the kids at the Dream Street Foundation, and I love my children more than life itself.

Airplanes have been a lifelong passion since the day I took my first lesson to overcome my fear of flying. My pilot's license says the FAA trusts me to fly single and multi-engine planes, a Learjet, a Citation jet, a seaplane, and a hot-air balloon. During my time in Aspen, I worked on quite a few search and rescue operations as a member of Air Rescue.

I love to cook, especially the recipes I learned from my two grandmothers, and I still try to practice the piano every day. My favorite pastime is making music surrounded by my family and friends. I do a great rendition of *The Best Things in Life Are Free*.

APPETIZERS &
HOR D' OEUVRES

Coquilles St. Jacques

Recipe from Arlene Grubman

1 cup dry white wine

1/2 tsp. salt

1 lb. shrimp

2 Tbsp. finely chopped onion

1/4 lb. sliced small mushrooms

1/4 cup butter (for sauce)

1/4 cup all purpose flour

1/2 cup heavy cream

2 tsp. lemon juice

1/3 cup grated Swiss cheese

1-2 Tbsp. parsley

1/2 cup soft bread crumbs

1 Tbsp. melted butter
(for topping)

parsley and lemon wedges

Bring wine to boil in small saucepan. Add salt and shrimp. Cover and simmer until just tender, about 4-5 minutes. Drain, reserving 1 cup liquid.

Sauté onion and mushrooms in butter until soft, in medium size pan. Remove from heat. Stir in flour until smooth, gradually stir in reserved liquid. Cook stirring constantly until sauce thickens and bubbles. About 1 minute. Stir in cream and lemon juice. Bring to boil. Remove from heat. If sauce is too thick, add more cream or wine. Taste and add more salt if necessary.

Add shrimp, cheese, parsley to sauce. Spoon into 4 buttered shells or individual soufflé dishes. Divide evenly.

Toss bread crumbs with melted butter. Sprinkle crumbs around edges of the shells. (You may freeze it at this point.)

Broil 4" to 6" from heat for 4 minutes, or until crumbs are brown and sauce bubbles. Garnish with parsley and lemon wedges. Makes 4 main courses or 6 to 8 appetizers.

Arlene

SALMON MOUSSE

Recipe from Marlene Kamin

Marlene and I were roommates at the University of Arizona. We once set our hair in rollers, rented a convertible and drove around Tucson until our hair was dry.

1 cup sour cream

1/2 cup mayonnaise

dash lemon juice

1 tsp. dill weed

1 tsp. horseradish, red or white

1-1/4 lb. of fresh cooked salmon (or 1 lb. can of salmon plus 1 small can)

1 package Knox gelatin

1/2 cup warm water

Dissolve gelatin in 1/2 cup of warm water.

Put all else into a blender and blend, then add gelatin mixture. Blend well.

Pour into well-oiled mold, or pour into serving bowl and refrigerate for several hours.

Serve with crackers or thinly sliced bread.

Marlene

Judy and Marlene

Smoked Trout Paté

Recipe from Marlene Kamin

This recipe can be whipped up in no time and it's fabulous!

2 Tbsp. finely chopped shallot

2 Tbsp. fresh lemon juice

1 8-oz. package cream cheese, softened

1/4 lb. smoked trout, discard skin

3 Tbsp. finely chopped fresh chives

salt and pepper

Stir together shallot, lemon juice, then with a spoon stir in cream cheese and trout.

Season with pepper and a little salt. Stir in chives.

Cover and chill. This will last 5 days in the fridge.

Serve with toast or crackers. This can also be used as a filling for Belgian endive leaves.

Marlene and Judy

SHRIMP CAKES WITH CHILI-LIME SAUCE

Recipe from author Marcia Sargent

16 uncooked large shrimp (approx 1 lb.) peeled and deveined

1 large egg

1 green onion, sliced

2 Tbsp. fresh lemon juice

1 Tbsp. Dijon mustard

1 Tbsp. minced fresh cilantro

1/4 tsp. salt

Black pepper and Tabasco Sauce to taste

2 cups panko (Japanese bread crumbs)

Peanut Oil

Chili-Lime Sauce (see recipe on opposite page)

Coarsely chop shrimp in processor.

Add egg, green onion, lemon juice, mustard, cilantro, salt, black pepper, and Tabasco Sauce. Blend using on/off turns.

Blend in 1 cup of panko.

Form mixture into 2" cakes. Roll cakes in remaining panko. Refrigerate on wax paper lined baking sheet at least 10 minutes. (Can be made up to 4 hours ahead. Cover and refrigerate.)

In a large skillet, heat 2 Tbsp. peanut oil over medium-high heat.

Fry cakes until golden brown on both sides and cooked through. Add more oil to skillet as needed.

Put a few spoonfuls of Chili-Lime Sauce onto a plate and top with 2 shrimp cakes.

Serve immediately.

CHILI-LIME SAUCE

Recipe from author Marcia Sargent

1/4 cup dry white wine

1/4 cup fresh lime juice

1 Tbsp. chopped peeled fresh ginger

1 Tbsp. minced shallot

1/3 cup whipping cream

2 Tbsp. chili-garlic sauce (available in the Asian foods section of many supermarkets)

6 Tbsp. unsalted butter, room temperature, cut into 1/2 inch pieces

Combine first 4 ingredients in a small saucepan. Boil over high heat until reduced by half, about 3 minutes.

Add cream and boil until reduced by half, about 2 minutes. Reduce heat to low.

Stir in chili-garlic sauce. Whisk in butter 1 piece at a time.

Make sure butter is melted before adding the next piece.

Marcia and Judy

Mom's Chopped Liver

Recipe from Arlene Grubman

1 lb. sautéed calves liver *

3 eggs, hard-boiled

1 onion, chopped

1 Tbsp. salt

1/4 tsp. pepper

Put above ingredients through a meat grinder.

Add 1/4 cup canola oil. Season with salt and pepper to taste.

Serve with crackers.

Heat oil in skillet. Add liver. Cook thoroughly and devein.

I'm not sure who taught my mother to make chopped liver. It was either Grandma Blanche (left) or Grandma Miriam. This photo of the three of them was taken at my father's fiftieth birthday party.

Shao Mai

I learned how to make these at a Chinese cooking class held in my Aspen kitchen. As an added attraction, the instructor's hair caught on fire! Fortunately, neither the instructor nor my kitchen suffered any serious damage, and the Shao Mai was smokin'!

1 lb. ground pork

1 carrot, chopped

2 green onions, chopped

3 leaves Chinese cabbage, chopped

4 water chestnuts (chopped) or substitute jicama

1 Tbsp. wine

1 Tbsp. soy sauce

1 tsp. salt

1 tsp. sugar

1 Tbsp. cornstarch

2 tsp. ginger (chopped)

wonton wrappers

Combine all ingredients except wonton wrappers in a bowl and mix thoroughly. Cut the wonton wrappers into 3" circles.

Place each wrapper in the palm of your hand and cup it loosely. Place 1 Tbsp. of the filling in the cup. Then, with your other hand, gather the sides of the wrapper around the filling, letting the wrapper pleat naturally.

Squeeze the middle gently to make sure the wrapper fits firmly against the filling and to give the dumpling a faintly wasp-waisted look. Tap the dumpling to flatten its bottom so that it can sit upright.

Place on an oiled plate, do not let them touch each other. Place in a steamer on a damp cloth (on an oiled plate) and steam for about 20 minutes over high heat.

These are generally served with a combination of soy sauce and black vinegar. These may be made ahead and covered with plastic for 2 to 3 hours.

Better than Shrimp Scampi

Recipe from Arlene Grubman

3 lbs. cooked shrimp

1/2 tsp. salt

1 clove garlic, minced

3/4 cup butter

1 cup bread crumbs, plus extra for sprinkling on top

4 tsp. minced parsley

1/2 cup sherry

1/8 tsp. white pepper

1/8 tsp. paprika

Cream together the butter, salt and garlic.

Add bread crumbs, parsley, sherry, white pepper and paprika.

Alternate butter mixture with layers of shrimp in a casserole or individual ramekins.

Top with bread crumbs.

Bake 10 to 15 minutes at 400°.

Arlene, 1929

STUFFED PORTOBELLO MUSHROOMS

Recipe from Andrea Bernard

2 Tbsp. olive oil, plus more for baking sheet

6 portobello mushrooms, stems removed and reserved

1/4 cup finely grated Parmesan cheese

1/4 cup grated Jack cheese

1/4 cup plain bread crumbs

3 Tbsp. chopped fresh parsley

3 Tbsp. chopped fresh chives

2 shallots, thinly sliced

1 lb. white mushrooms, sliced

1/2 cup dry white wine

1/2 cup whipping cream

1 tsp. coarse salt

1/4 tsp. freshly ground pepper

Preheat oven to 350°.

Lightly oil a rimmed baking sheet. Arrange portobello mushroom caps, gill sides down, on sheet. Bake 20 to 25 minutes, until tender. Transfer to a plate to cool.

Preheat broiler.

Stir together Parmesan and Jack cheese, bread crumbs, 1 Tbsp. parsley, 1 Tbsp. chives and 1 Tbsp. oil. Set aside. Chop portobello stems into 1/2" pieces. Heat remaining tablespoon oil in a large skillet over medium heat until hot.

Add shallots, cook stirring until softened, about 2 minutes. Add sliced mushrooms and chopped stems. Cook, stirring occasionally, until tender, 6 to 7 minutes.

Add wine, cook until most of the liquid has evaporated, about 2 minutes. Stir in cream, remaining parsley and chives. Season with salt and pepper. Remove from heat.

Arrange mushroom caps, gill sides up, on a baking sheet. Fill mushrooms caps with mushroom mixture. Top with crumb mixture. Broil until golden brown, about 2 minutes. Serves 6.

Judy and Andrea

Judy's Stuffed Mushrooms

1-1/4 lb. fresh mushrooms

1-1/2 Tbsp. chopped
scallions or chives

1 Tbsp. butter

6 oz. whipping cream

1-1/2 Tbsp. sherry

1/2 tsp. salt

1/8 tsp. pepper

Clean mushrooms. Remove stems and chop finely. Set aside 15 to 20 mushroom caps.

Chop the remaining mushrooms. Sauté chopped mushrooms and scallions in the butter.

Add cream, sherry, salt and pepper.

Cook until mixture thickens, about 5 minutes.

Fill mushroom caps that were set aside.

Refrigerate until ready to broil. Broil until bubbling, about 3-5 minutes.

Me and my Mom in Brooklyn.

SPINACH BALLS

Recipe from Arlene Grubman

2 10-oz. pkgs. frozen chopped spinach, thawed, squeeze dry

2 cups herb stuffing mix, crushed

1 cup firmly packed Parmesan cheese

1/2 cup (1 stick) butter, melted

4 small green onions finely chopped

3 eggs

dash of fresh nutmeg

For the sauce:

1/2 cup dry mustard

1/2 cup white vinegar

1/4 cup sugar

1 egg yolk

Combine all ingredients in large bowl, mix well. Shape into 1" balls. Cover and refrigerate, or freeze until ready to bake. Preheat oven to 350°. Set balls on ungreased cookie sheet. Bake 10 to 15 minutes, until golden brown. Makes 70 balls.

Serve with the following sauce:
Combine mustard and vinegar in small bowl. Cover and let stand at room temperature for about 4 hours.

Mix sugar and egg yolk in small saucepan. Add mustard mixture and cook over low heat. Stir constantly until slightly thickened.

Cover and chill. Serve at room temperature.

Me and my Mom in Grandma Blanche and Grandpa Sam's backyard on Albers Street.

SPINACH DIP

Recipe from Mary Ann Greene

2 onions, chopped

2 tomatoes, peeled, seeded and chopped

1 4-oz. can Ortega chopped green chiles

2 packages chopped frozen spinach, thawed and squeezed dry

3 cups grated cheese (Can use a mixture of sharp cheddar or Monterey jack)

1 8-oz. pkg. cream cheese, cut in small pieces

1/2 cup half and half

1 Tbsp. red wine vinegar

salt and pepper to taste

Sauté onions in a small amount of oil for 4 to 5 minutes.

Add tomatoes and chiles and cook for 1 minute longer.

Transfer to a bowl and mix in remaining ingredients. Bake at 375° until bubbly.

Serve with tortilla chips.

This dish can be made well in advance.

Mary Ann Greene was my neighbor in Aspen. She was an extraordinary hostess!

Judy's White Bean Bruschetta

1 can cannellini beans,
drained and rinsed

1 or 2 cloves garlic, mashed

1/4 cup extra virgin olive oil

2 Tbsp. minced basil

Salt and pepper to taste

Mash ingredients together.

Serve with toasted ciabatta or other rustic bread.

Judy

Judy's Crab Cakes

I've had crab cakes in many restaurants, but I think these are the best. I have found that this particular combination of ingredients makes the best crab cakes. Adjust the amount of herbs and seasonings to your own taste.

Fresh crab meat

Celery

Chives

Old Bay seasoning

Fresh marjoram

Lemon juice

Salt & pepper

Mayonnaise

Egg white

Bread crumbs

Mix fresh crab meat with minced celery, chives, Old Bay seasoning, fresh marjoram, lemon juice, salt & pepper, mayonnaise, egg white and some bread crumbs .

Shape into patties.

Dip into additional bread crumbs to coat the patty.

Sauté in canola oil until brown on both sides.

Drain on paper towels.

Anna and Emma

Judy's Caviar-Stuffed Potatoes

Everyone in the family loves these.

12 small scrubbed unpeeled new potatoes, boiled (do not overcook)

1/2 cup sour cream

1 2-oz. tin of caviar

2 hard-cooked egg yolks, sieved

Using a teaspoon or small melon scoop, hollow out the top of each boiled potato.

Fill each hollow with a teaspoon of sour cream, top with a dab of caviar and sprinkle with sieved yolk.

Serve potatoes cold. Serves 6.

Anna and Emma

Oven Roasted Tomatoes
with Fresh Thyme

Judy's special recipe

6-8 tomatoes, preferably heirloom (any color), or you can use a mixture of heirloom and other varieties

4 cloves fresh garlic, chopped

8 sprigs of thyme, leaves removed

1/2 cup extra virgin olive oil

2 Tbsp. sherry or balsamic vinegar

salt and freshly ground pepper

Preheat oven to 250°.

Cut tomatoes in half, gently squeeze to remove seeds. Cut each half into 3 to 4 pieces.

Combine tomatoes, garlic, thyme, olive oil and vinegar in a bowl, then pour into prepared dish.

Generously season with salt and freshly ground pepper.

Bake for 2-1/2 to 3 hours.

This recipe is easy and fabulous. Serve hot or at room temperature with crusty bread or crackers as an appetizer. This dish can be prepared early in the day.

Emily, Judy and Cristiana
Carnival in Venice 2011.

BRIE WITH APRICOT JAM

Recipe from Marlene Kamin's mother,
Ellie Kamm

1/2 cup apricot jam

1 Tbsp. brandy

1 Tbsp. lemon juice

1/8 tsp. ground cinnamon

1 piece Brie cheese
(about 1/2 lb.)

thin baguette slices
or water crackers

Mix jam, brandy, lemon juice and cinnamon in a shallow microwave-safe serving dish just large enough to also hold the Brie.

Cover apricot sauce and heat in a microwave oven at full power until sauce begins to bubble, 1 to 1-1/2 minutes.

Set Brie in apricot sauce.

Return to microwave oven and cook, uncovered, until the cheese is hot and slightly melted, about 1 minute.

Check at 20-second intervals.

Scoop cheese and apricot sauce onto baguette slices.

Judy and Marlene

CHILE CHEESE CUBES

10 eggs

1/2 cup all-purpose flour

1 tsp. baking powder

4 cups (16 oz.) shredded Monterey jack cheese

1 pint cottage cheese

2 4-oz. cans mild green chilies, drained, seeded and chopped

1/4 tsp. salt

Butter a 9" x 13" x 2" baking dish. In large bowl beat eggs lightly. In a separate bowl, combine flour, baking powder, and salt.

Add to eggs and mix well. Fold in cheeses and add chilies. Mix until blended. Pour into baking dish.

Bake in 400° oven for 15 minutes. Reduce heat to 350°and bake additional 35 to 40 minutes. Remove from oven. Let stand 10 minutes.

Cut into small squares. Serve hot.

Can be made early in the day. Refrigerate, then put in the oven just before your company is due to arrive.

Judy, Carnival in Venice 2011.

CHEESE APPETIZERS THREE WAYS

My children love these.

PARMESAN ONION CANAPE

Finely chop 1 onion. Add about 1/2 cup of mayo and 1/2 cup of graded Parmesan cheese. Adjust amount to your taste. Spread on melba rounds and broil until brown. About 5 minutes.

SWISS DELIGHTS

Whisk stiffly 2 egg whites. Mix in 2-1/2 oz. grated gruyere cheese and 2-1/2 oz. grated mozzarella cheese. Add 1 Tbsp. minced parsley and a small pinch of cayenne pepper. Form the mixture into little balls, coat with egg and bread crumbs. Fry in hot oil. Drain on paper towels. Serve immediately.

CHEESE TRAY

Decorate with:
Walnut halves, whole almonds, dried apricots, fresh figs (cut in half), strawberries, fruit paste or unusual syrups.

Steven and Carrie with Alfie as Santa Claus.

SOUPS

CHICKEN SOUP

Recipe from Arlene Grubman

1 chicken, cut in pieces

1 onion, cut into quarters

3 carrots, cut into two-inch lengths

3 celery stalks, cut into two-inch lengths

1 small parsnip

generous amount of parsley sprigs

salt and pepper to taste

Put ingredients into a large pot. Add enough cold water to cover by 1".

Bring to a boil, then reduce heat to a low simmer.

Occasionally skim off the foam that rises to the top. Cook about 1 hour.

Discard parsley, and cool until fat rises to the surface. Skim off fat. Heat, and serve with noodles or matzo balls.

Arlene Grubman

Matzo Balls

Recipe from Grandma Blanche

matzo meal
2 eggs
1/2 tsp. salt

Put 1 cup Matzo Meal in bowl. Add 1 cup boiling water and mix well.

Separate 2 eggs. Fold into matzo meal mixture.

Beat well and add 1/2 tsp. salt.

Stiffly beat egg whites. Fold into mixture.

Put in refrigerator until needed.

Make balls. Cook in simmering water, about 1/2 hour.

Partially cover the pot while the matzo balls are cooking.

Blanche

After she was orphaned as a teenager, Grandma Blanche supported herself by playing the piano in silent movie theaters.

JUDY'S EASY GAZPACHO

1 English cucumber

1/2 mild red onion

1 avocado

1 tsp. dried oregano

3 Tbsp. olive oil

2 Tbsp. wine vinegar

4 cups tomato juice

Tabasco sauce to taste

fresh oregano or cilantro

sour cream (optional)

Dice cucumber and onion. Put in large bowl with everything else except avocado.

Stir, add Tabasco sauce to your liking (approx. 10 drops).

Chill. When ready to serve, top with diced avocado and garnish with sour cream (if desired) and fresh oregano or cilantro.

Mom and I always had great fun together.

Avocado Soup

I have been making this for years. It's very rich. Servings should be small.

1 13-3/4-oz. can chicken broth

2 medium avocados, seeded, peeled, and cut into chunks

2 Tbsp. dry sherry

1/2 tsp. salt

1/4 tsp. onion powder

1/8 tsp. dried dill weed

3/4 cup light cream

In blender container combine chicken broth, avocado chunks, dry sherry, salt, onion powder and dill weed.

Cover; blend until mixture is smooth. Stir in light cream.

Turn into refrigerator container.

Cover; chill well.

Top each serving with slices of avocado or dollops of sour cream, if desired.

Parker

Beckett

Pappa Al Pomodoro
Tuscan Tomato-Bread Soup

Billy sent me this recipe after our trip to Italy.

2 large red onions, finely chopped

1/3 cup olive oil, plus additional extra-virgin olive oil for drizzling

4-5 garlic cloves, minced

1-1/2 cups dry white wine

2 (28 oz.) cans whole or crushed San Marzano tomatoes

3-1/2 cups water

1-1/2 cups coarsely chopped fresh basil, plus additional for sprinkling

8 cups day-old country bread, crust removed and cut into 1-inch cubes

salt and pepper to taste

Parmesan cheese for sprinkling

In a large heavy pot cook onions in olive oil over moderate heat for 2 minutes, stirring often.

Add garlic and continue to cook until onions are soft and beginning to brown.

Raise heat to medium-high.

Add wine and cook until wine has reduced to 1/2 cup. Add tomatoes, water and half of the basil.

Bring mixture to a gentle simmer and cook for 15 minutes.

Reduce heat to low and add bread. Cook, stirring occasionally for 10 minutes.

Add salt and pepper to taste. Add remaining basil and more water if desired.

Serve drizzled with extra-virgin olive oil and grated Parmesan cheese.

Some of the best times of my life have been spent with my brother and sister.

TUSCAN TOMATO SOUP

1/4 cup olive oil

4 Tbsp. butter

4 carrots, peeled and finely diced

4 stalks celery, finely diced

6 leaves fresh basil

3 medium onions, finely diced

5 14-oz. cans Italian tomatoes

1 can (14-1/2 oz.) chicken broth

2 Tbsp. sugar

2 Tbsp. tomato paste

1/2 cup finely chopped flat-leaf parsley

salt and fresh ground pepper to taste

Heat oil and butter in a heavy pot.

Cook carrots, celery, and onions until very tender.

Add tomatoes, chicken broth, sugar, and tomato paste, and continue cooking over moderate heat for 25 to 30 minutes.

Stir in parsley and basil, and season with salt and pepper.

Cook about 1 minute more.

Serve hot.

Cuban Black Bean Soup

Recipe from Maria Braun

3-4 15-oz. cans black beans, drained and rinsed

2 Tbsp. olive oil

1 small onion, chopped

2 garlic cloves, chopped

1 tsp. dried oregano

1 tsp. chili powder

1/2 tsp. ground cumin

4 cups (or more) low sodium chicken broth

1 14-oz. can diced tomatoes in juice

2 Tbsp. sherry

1/2 cup fresh cilantro, chopped

Ingredients for Garnish:

fresh tomato salsa

chopped fresh cilantro

sour cream

guacamole

Heat olive oil in a heavy large pot over medium heat. Add onion, garlic, oregano, chili powder and cumin.

Cook until onion is translucent, stirring frequently, about 5 minutes.

Add chicken broth, tomatoes with juice, and beans. Bring to boil. Reduce heat and simmer 15 minutes.

Using an immersion blender, coarsely puree soup. Add more broth if needed.

Add sherry and simmer 2 minutes. Stir in chopped cilantro. Season to taste with salt and pepper.

Serve with salsa, chopped cilantro, sour cream, and guacamole.

Maria Braun

GREEN SALADS &
MAIN COURSE SALADS

CAESAR SALAD

Recipe from Lynn and Carl Hanauer

Romaine lettuce

Dressing:

1/3 cup vinegar

1/2 cup extra virgin olive oil

1 Tbsp. lemon juice

1 tsp. Worcestershire sauce (approx.)

1 Tbsp. mayonnaise

1/2 tsp. Dijon mustard

2 cloves of garlic, crushed

black pepper

optional - mash anchovies in a little olive oil

Put all the above ingredients in a small glass jar (one that will accommodate the ingredients) and shake well.

Croutons:
Rub a garlic clove over toasted bread.

To Assemble Salad:
Put dry greens and croutons in a salad bowl. Add dressing and toss.

Add Parmesan cheese (a lot). Toss again.

Carl and Lynn at Clivden.

Green Salad
with Hot Brie Dressing

Recipe from a neighbor in Aspen

It's yummy!

Romaine lettuce

garlic croutons

Hot Dressing:

1/2 cup olive oil

4 tsp. minced shallot

2 tsp. minced garlic

1/2 cup sherry wine vinegar

2 Tbsp. fresh lemon juice

4 tsp. Dijon mustard

10 ounces ripe Brie cheese, rind removed, cut into small pieces, room temperature

Fresh ground pepper

Tear lettuce into bite-size pieces.

Toss with garlic croutons in large bowl.

Toss hot dressing with lettuce and serve.

Serves 8.

For Hot Dressing:
Warm olive oil in heavy skillet over low heat for 10 minutes.

Add shallot and garlic and cook until translucent, stirring occasionally, about 5 minutes.

Blend in vinegar, lemon juice and mustard. Add cheese and stir until smooth. Season with pepper.

MEDITERRANEAN SALAD

Recipe from Lynn Hanauer

1 head Romaine, torn
into bite-size pieces

3 tomatoes, chopped

1 cucumber, peeled and diced

1 cup black olives, pitted

4 oz. Feta cheese, crumbled

1/2 cup olive oil

1/4 cup red wine vinegar

3/4 tsp. dried oregano,
crumbled

Combine lettuce, tomatoes, cucumber, olives and cheese in salad bowl.

Whisk together olive oil, vinegar and oregano.

Season to taste with salt and pepper.

Pour dressing over salad and toss. Serves 4.

Judy and Lynn, 1965. My parent's front yard in Studio City.

WOODS LAKE SALAD DRESSING

Recipe from Annie Denver

5 Tbsp. olive oil

3 Tbsp. cider vinegar

1 Tbsp. pure maple syrup

1 Tbsp. Dijon mustard

1-1/2 tsp. dill weed

1-1/2 tsp. tarragon

fresh ground black pepper

Whisk all ingredients together.

Annie and Judy

Camping with the Denvers at Woods Lake, Colorado.

ENDIVE SALAD
WITH PEARS, WALNUTS & ROQUEFORT

I make this salad at least once a week. It's our favorite.

2 Tbsp. balsamic vinegar
1/4 tsp. salt
1/4 tsp. freshly ground pepper
1/4 cup extra-virgin olive oil
2 cups arugula
2 large heads endive sliced into 1/2 inch pieces
1 pear, cored and cubed
1/2 cup toasted walnut halves
1/2 cup crumbled Roquefort cheese

In a small bowl, whisk together vinegar, salt and pepper. Slowly whisk in oil; set aside.

In a medium bowl, combine arugula, cut-up endive, pears, walnuts, and cheese.

Drizzle with dressing, gently toss to coat evenly.

Serve immediately.

Judy

Jicama, Mandarin Orange & Green Bean Salad

Recipe from Billy

This colorful salad from my brother, Billy, is great with a Mexican-themed menu.

2 cups green beans, sliced

1 large jicama, peeled and julienned (about 2 cups)

3 8-oz. cans mandarin orange sections, drained

10 leaves of lettuce

mint orange-walnut vinaigrette (see recipe on opposite page)

In a medium saucepan, cook green beans in boiling salted water until tender-crisp, 6 to 8 minutes.

Drain, and plunge into ice water to stop cooking process. Drain again and set aside. In a large bowl combine green beans, jicama, and orange sections.

Pour dressing over salad mixture and gently stir to coat. Let marinate in refrigerator 30 minutes.

Arrange lettuce leaves on serving plates. With a slotted spoon, set an equal amount of vegetable mixture onto each lettuce leaf.

Billy and Lenny at Marcia's 60th birthday party.

MINT ORANGE-WALNUT VINAIGRETTE

Recipe from Billy

2 Tbsp. frozen orange juice concentrate, thawed

1/3 cup white wine vinegar

2/3 cup walnut oil or 1/3 cup each of walnut oil and canola oil

1/3 cup fresh mint leaves, minced

1 jalapeno chile, finely minced (take precautions when cutting jalapeno)

In a medium bowl, combine all ingredients. Makes about 1-1/2 cups of dressing.

Mathew and Emily (top)
Mathew, Emily, and Billy at the Braun Ranch. (bottom)

Lenny's Famous House Chopped Salad

with MayTag Blue Cheese Dressing

1-2 bags of triple washed Romaine lettuce

4-6 green onions (scallions), chopped

1-2 cups frozen peas, blanch in boiling water for about 3-4 minutes then dip in ice bath, drain and pat dry

6-7 stalks hearts of palm, sliced 1/4" thick

1 can quartered artichokes packed in WATER (cut each quarter in half again)

5-6 fresh mushrooms, sliced thin

1/2 of an English cucumber, diced and seeds removed

2 avocados, cut into small chunks

Place the ingredients in a big salad bowl and toss with dressing (see recipe on next page).

Billy, Judy, Wes and Lenny at The Great Wall

MayTag Blue Cheese Dressing

3 Tbsp. mayonnaise
(Best Foods is best!)

1-1/2 tsp. Colman's
dry mustard

2-3 cloves of fresh crushed
pressed garlic

6 oz. MayTag blue cheese (do
not buy pre-crumbled package)

1/2 tsp. Worcestershire sauce

1/2 cup extra virgin olive oil
(or more if needed)

1/4 cup regular olive oil

sea salt, to taste

fresh ground pepper, to taste

In a medium bowl, mix the mayo, mustard and Worcestershire sauce with a FORK.

Then add the garlic and break up chunks of the blue cheese into the bowl.

Mix with the fork for a minute or two, but do not try to break down the cheese completely. It should be a thick paste with small chunks of blue cheese.

Make a hole in the center of this mixture.

Add both olive oils slowly and mix with the fork. You can add additional Extra Virgin Olive Oil if needed.

Dressing should be the consistency of a thick pea soup. Add salt and pepper to taste.

Judy

Asian Coleslaw

Dressing:

1/4 cup fresh lime juice

1/4 cup minced shallot

1 Tbsp. soy sauce

1-1/2 Tbsp. minced peeled fresh ginger

2 tsp. minced garlic

1 Tbsp. honey

2 tsp. Thai red curry paste (available in Asian markets and specialty food shops)

1 Tbsp. dark sesame oil (Asian)

1/2 cup peanut, soy or canola oil

Salad:

5 cups thinly sliced Napa cabbage (about 1/2 lb.)

1-1/2 cups julienne strips carrot (about 2 carrots)

1/2 cup thinly sliced scallion

1/4 cup chopped fresh cilantro

2 Tbsp. coarsely chopped unsalted roasted peanuts

1 Tbsp. sesame seeds, toasted lightly

2 tsp. coarse salt

1/8 tsp. freshly ground black pepper

Dressing:

In a large bowl, whisk together the following ingredients: fresh lime juice, minced shallot, soy sauce, fresh ginger, garlic, honey, Thai red curry paste, dark sesame oil, peanut, soy or canola oil.

Salad:

Add these remaining ingredients to dressing and toss well: Napa cabbage, carrots, scallion, fresh cilantro, unsalted roasted peanuts, sesame seeds, toasted lightly, salt, and pepper.

Let stand 10 minutes before serving.
Makes 6 servings.

Judy

Minestrone Salad

8 oz. Penne or other small-size pasta

4 Tbsp. extra virgin olive oil

1 onion, diced

2 cloves garlic, minced

1 carrot, peeled and diced

1 zucchini, diced

4 oz. green beans, cut into 1" pieces

1-1/4 cups fresh or frozen corn kernels

freshly ground pepper

2 Tbsp. balsamic vinegar

1 15-oz. can cannellini beans, rinsed and drained

1 lb. assorted tomatoes, chopped

Parmesan cheese

fresh basil leaves, chopped

Cook pasta in salted water until al dente. Drain, and rinse under cold water; set aside.

Heat 2 Tbsp. of olive oil in large skillet over medium heat. Add onion and garlic, cook until they begin to soften, about 2 minutes.

Add carrot and cook until it softens, about 4 minutes. Add zucchini, green beans, and corn.

Cook until vegetables are tender, stirring occasionally. Season with salt and pepper.

Transfer to a bowl to cool. Stir in remaining 2 Tbsp. of olive oil, vinegar, beans, tomatoes, and pasta.

Add more salt and pepper, if needed. Add Parmesan cheese and fresh basil. Serve chilled or at room temperature.

Billy

PANZANELLA SALAD

1 clove garlic,
peeled and minced

1 lb. cherry tomatoes, halved

1/2 cup thinly sliced red onion

5 Tbsp. extra virgin olive oil

3 Tbsp. red wine vinegar

coarse salt and freshly
ground pepper

1/2 loaf crusty Italian bread

1 English cucumber,
peeled and diced large

cubed fresh mozzarella
or bocconcini

10 to 15 fresh basil leaves,
thinly sliced

Place tomatoes, onion and garlic in a large non-reactive bowl.

Drizzle the oil and vinegar over the vegetable mixture.

Season with salt and pepper. Toss, let stand in a cool place for one hour or more.

Place the bread on a hot grill or under a heated broiler, until both sides are slightly charred, 2 to 3 minutes.

Remove from heat, rub with garlic if desired.

Tear bread into bite-size chunks. When ready to serve, add the cucumbers, mozzarella, basil, and bread to the tomatoes.

Toss. Adjust the seasoning with salt and pepper.

MEXICAN SALAD

Lettuce

tomato

avocado

tortilla chips

cheddar cheese

ground turkey

onion

kidney beans

Thousand Island
or French dressing

Layer in a large bowl: Lettuce, tomato, avocado, and crumbled tortilla chips.

Put cheddar cheese on top. In a frying pan, sauté ground turkey, onion, kidney beans.

When thoroughly cooked, pour on top of cheddar cheese and let stand for a minute to melt the cheese a little.

Toss with Thousand Island or French dressing.

ASIAN BARBECUE CHICKEN SALAD

Wes's mother got this recipe from her La Cañada neighbor.

Asian Barbeque Sauce:

1/3 cup hoisin sauce

1/4 cup olive oil

1 Tbsp. honey

1 Tbsp. soy sauce

1 tsp. minced fresh ginger

1 garlic clove, minced

Salad:

4-5 skinless boneless chicken breasts, cooked and brushed with the barbecue sauce

8 cups chopped Romaine lettuce (about 1 large head)

6 plum tomatoes, quartered lengthwise

1 Tbsp. sesame seeds, toasted

1-1/2 cups garlic Croutons

Dressing:

1/4 cup sugar

1/4 cup rice vinegar

1/4 cup chopped onion

3/4 tsp. dry mustard powder

1/2 cup canola oil

1-1/2 tsp. poppy seeds

Dressing:

Whisk sugar, rice vinegar, onion and mustard powder in small bowl to blend.

Gradually whisk in oil.

Stir in poppy seeds.

Season with salt and pepper to taste. Cover and refrigerate.

Asian Barbecue Sauce:

Whisk hoisin sauce, oil, honey, soy sauce, ginger, and garlic in small bowl to blend.

Cover and refrigerate.

For Salad:

Cut chicken crosswise into 1/2" thick strips.

Place lettuce in large bowl.

Toss with 1/2 cup dressing. Add croutons, and toss again.

Divide lettuce mixture among 4 plates. Garnish with tomatoes and grilled chicken strips.

Drizzle chicken with barbecue sauce.

Sprinkle with toasted sesame seeds and serve.

Oriental Pasta Salad

8 oz. curly instant chukka soba noodles (or linguini)

1/2 cup thawed apple juice concentrate

1/2 cup water chestnuts

1 head green cabbage, sliced thin, about 12 cups

2 cups chopped green onions

8 whole green onions for garnish

Dressing:

1/2 cup rice vinegar

3 Tbsp. dark sesame oil

1 tsp. fresh ginger, peeled and minced

1/2 tsp. salt

1 tsp. freshly ground pepper

1 garlic clove, minced, about 1 tsp.

1 tsp. hot sesame oil

Combine all dressing ingredients in a small bowl and mix well.

Bring water to a boil. Cook soba noodles or linguini as directed on package directions.

Drain thoroughly and transfer to a large bowl.

Add dressing and mix well. Add cabbage and onions and mix thoroughly.

Cover and refrigerate overnight.

Makes 8 servings, 230 calories each.

Judy's Easy Chinese Chicken Salad

2 cups chicken,
cooked and shredded

1 bunch green onions, thinly
sliced on a diagonal

2 cups shredded lettuce

1/4 cup sesame seeds, toasted

2 cups Mai Fun noodles (or
bean threads)

oil for frying noodles

Dressing:

5 Tbsp. plum sauce

1 tsp. dry mustard

2 Tbsp. dark sesame oil

2 Tbsp. rice vinegar

2 Tbsp. sugar

Prepare chicken and greens.

Toast sesame seeds. Combine ingredients for dressing (this can be done in advance).

Just prior to serving, heat oil in heavy skillet.

Stir fry Mai Fun noodles in hot oil until crisp, but still white.

DO NOT ALLOW THEM TO BROWN!

Toss fried noodles with dressing, chicken and greens. Serve immediately.

THE EGG & THE EYE CURRIED CHICKEN SALAD

This combination restaurant/art gallery used to be across from the L.A. County Museum. It closed many years ago, but I was lucky enough to get this recipe from one of the waiters.

4-5 chicken breasts, halved

1/2 cup chopped celery

1/2 cup coarsely cut prunes

1/2 cup golden raisins

1/2 cup cooked or canned seedless white grapes

4 papayas

lettuce leaves

tomato wedges

Curry Dressing:

1 cup whipping cream

1/3 cup mayonnaise

curry powder, to taste (I use a lot)

salt, pepper

Cook chicken in boiling salted water until tender. Drain and cool. Cut into chunks.

Combine chicken with celery, prunes, raisins, grapes, and curry dressing. Toss to mix well. Chill.

Cut papayas into halves and remove seeds. Spoon chicken salad into papaya cavities.

Serve on lettuce leaf and garnish with tomato wedges.

Dressing:
Whisk together whipping cream, mayonnaise, and curry powder to taste until smooth.

Season to taste with salt and pepper.

POULTRY & FISH

Best Chicken Cacciatore

Recipe from Arlene Grubman

3 lbs. chicken
(breast, legs, thighs)

3/4 cup all purpose flour

1 tsp. salt

1/4 tsp. pepper

1/3 cup olive oil
(not extra virgin)

1 large onion, chopped, about
1 cup

1 clove garlic, minced

1 2-lb. can Italian tomatoes

1 Tbsp. sugar

1 tsp. dry basil

1/2 tsp. dry thyme

1 green pepper, halved,
seeded and sliced

Shake the chicken with flour, salt and pepper in a plastic bag to coat well.

Brown chicken a few pieces at a time in the oil in a large skillet. Remove from pan.

Stir onion and garlic into drippings in pan and sauté until soft.

Stir in tomatoes, sugar, basil and thyme. Bring to a boil.

Return chicken to pan. Spoon some of the tomato sauce over chicken.

Lay sliced peppers on top and cover pan.

Simmer until tender, basting several times with sauce in pan.

Delicious served with spaghetti, or just plain white rice. Really great, even for company.

Arlene and Judy

Sautéed Chicken
with Apples & Brandy

4 chicken breasts, halved

3-4 Tbsp. unsalted butter

2 large shallots, minced

1/4 cup plus 1 Tbsp. Calvados or apple brandy

1/2 granny smith or other tart green apple, pared, cored, cut into 1/4" slices

salt

freshly ground pepper

1/3 cup chicken broth

1/4 cup whipping cream

Brown chicken breasts in butter.

Sprinkle with shallots and 1 tablespoon of brandy.

Cook until chicken is done.

Remove chicken to platter, sprinkle with salt and pepper.

Keep warm. Pour 1/4 cup brandy into skillet.

Boil until reduced by half. Add chicken broth, cream and apple.

Boil until apple is tender and sauce is thickened. Taste and adjust the seasonings.

Poor sauce over the chicken before serving. Makes 4 servings.

Judy in front of Grandma Blanche's and Grandpa Sam's house.

LEMON CHICKEN

Recipe is from my sister Patty's friend Kippy

4 whole chicken breasts

1 cup flour - for dipping breasts before batter

4 cups oil heated to 350°

Marinade:

1 Tbsp. light soy sauce

1/4 Tbsp. sesame seed oil

1 tsp. salt

1 Tbsp. sherry

Batter for deep frying:

1/2 cup flour

1/2 tsp. baking soda

2 tsp. oil

1/2 tsp. salt

3/4 cup water

Lemon Sauce:

1 Tbsp. oil

1 cup sugar

1/2 cup fresh lemon juice

1/2 cup water

3 tsp. soy sauce

salt to taste

1 whole grated lemon rind

cornstarch to thicken

Marinade:

Mix ingredients together in a bowl big enough to hold chicken pieces.

Batter for deep frying:

Sift together flour, baking soda and salt. Add water and oil. Beat until well blended.

Lemon Sauce:

In a small saucepan mix oil, sugar, lemon juice, water, soy sauce and salt. Mix well and boil 5 minutes. Mix cornstarch with water and add to thicken sauce. When sauce has thickened, add grated lemon rind.

Cooking Instructions:

Cut chicken breasts in half. Bone and pound to flatten slightly. Place in bowl and cover with marinade. Let stand for 15 minutes.

Roll marinated chicken in flour, then dip in batter. Fry chicken until golden brown, about 10 minutes in 350° oil. Oil should be deep enough to cover chicken. Drain on a paper towel and keep warm.

Place chicken on serving platter. Pour lemon sauce over chicken and serve. Makes 4 servings.

CRANBERRY CHICKEN

Recipe from Grandma Blanche

3-4 pounds chicken pieces

1 1-lb. can whole cranberry sauce

1 envelope onion soup mix

1 8-oz. bottle French dressing

Place chicken pieces in a 2 inch deep pan.

Mix cranberry sauce, soup mix and French dressing together.

Pour over chicken and marinate a couple of hours, turning chicken occasionally.

Bake at 350° uncovered until done.

Serve with cooked white rice. Makes 6 to 8 servings.

Grandma Blanche's Italian Chicken

2 cans tomato soup

1 can tomato sauce

1 bay leaf

sweet pepper flakes

Italian seasoning

garlic

1 Tbsp. sugar

butter

salt and pepper

onions, sliced

chicken

Combine in a saucepan the tomato soup, tomato sauce, bay leaf, sweet pepper flakes, Italian seasoning, garlic, sugar, butter, salt, and pepper. Heat above ingredients.

Line the bottom of a pan with lots of thinly sliced onions. Dip chicken pieces in sauce.

Lay on top of sliced onions. Pour extra sauce over chicken.

Bake at 350° for 1 hour.

Serve with rice or noodles. Mix them with the tomato sauce.

Judy

CRISP CHICKEN

Recipe from Grandma Blanche

All her grandchildren love this recipe.

Chicken (breast, thighs, legs)
Kellogg's corn flake crumbs
1/2 pint sour cream
2 Tbsp. lemon juice
2 Tbsp. Worcestershire sauce
1 tsp. celery salt
1/2 tsp. garlic salt
1 tsp. paprika

Stir sour cream, lemon juice, Worcestershire sauce, celery salt, garlic salt, and paprika together.

Dip chicken in sour cream mixture, then in corn flake crumbs. Put chicken in a casserole. Drizzle a little melted butter over chicken.

Bake uncovered in 350° oven until done.

Grandma Blanche

SESAME COATED CHICKEN
WITH HONEY SAUCE

1 cup real mayonnaise

2 tsp. dry mustard

2 tsp. minced onion

1/2 cup bread crumbs

1/4 cup sesame seeds

4 boneless, skinless chicken breast, halved

Honey Sauce:

1 cup of real mayonnaise

1/4 cup of honey

Mix first 3 ingredients, set aside.

Mix bread crumbs with sesame seeds.

Coat chicken with mayonnaise mixture, then coat with crumb mixture.

Place on baking sheet.

Bake in 350° until done, approximately 30 minutes.

For the Honey Sauce, mix 1 cup of mayonnaise with 1/4 cup of honey.

Serve hot with honey sauce.

TURKEY BREAST

1/2 turkey breast

brush with olive oil

season with Lawrey's
seasoned salt

8-10 large rosemary sprigs

Preheat oven to 350°.

Lay turkey breast on top of rosemary sprigs.

Tuck extra rosemary between skin and breast meat. Place into oiled baking dish.

Cover loosely with aluminum foil.

Bake for 1 hour at 350°.

Remove foil and continue baking until done.

Total baking time is approximately 1-1/2 hours.

Lenny's Sea Bass

Recipe from Lenny Roberts

Simply delicious!

4 cups East-West Fat-Free Sweet Ginger Teriyaki Marinade

1/4 cup East-West Fat-Free Spicy Ginger Teriyaki Marinade (seeds strained out)

1 Tbsp. fresh grated ginger

1 clove fresh sliced garlic

2 Tbsp. dark brown sugar

1 Tbsp. honey

Place the ingredients into a saucepot and simmer for 1 hour. Remove from heat and let cool.

Strain to be sure to remove garlic slices.

Preheat your grill.

Place sea bass on grill only after it is well heated. When you are ready to turn fish over, brush it with the sauce.

Brush other side with sauce the last 2 minutes of grilling.

To avoid contamination, be sure that the sauce and utensils used to baste the raw fish do not come into contact with the finished food.

You can also use this sauce on salmon.

Lenny

Hot Shrimp

Recipe from Arlene Grubman

1-1/2 lbs. cooked, cleaned shrimp

1/2 lb. sweet butter

1/2 bottle Heinz chili sauce

1/8 cup catsup

juice of 1/4 lemon

2 tsp. paprika

1/2 tsp. salt

1/2 large bunch parsley, chopped

1/2 large bunch chives, finely chopped

bread crumbs

Place shrimp into individual ramekins or into a large flat souffle or casserole dish.

Cover with the following mixture of sweet butter, chili sauce, catsup, lemon, paprika, salt, parsley, and chives.

Sprinkle generously with bread crumbs.

Bake in 350° preheated oven about 15 minutes or under broiler for 10 minutes.

Just great as an hors d'oeuvres. Makes 6 servings.

Arlene

Island Fried Fish

Recipe from Arlene Grubman

This fish is dipped in batter for a crisp, golden crust and served with hot pineapple sauce.

2-1/2 to 3 lbs. fillet of sole

1/2 cup soy sauce

1/2 cup flour

1/4 cup cornstarch

about 1 cup milk

1 egg

3 tsp. baking powder

1 tsp. salt

1/2 tsp. pepper

2 20-oz. cans pineapple chunks in syrup

3/4 cup sugar

canola oil

Wash the fish, pat dry and cut into pieces about 1-1/2" square. Marinate in the soy sauce for 20 to 30 minutes, turning once or twice.

Combine flour, cornstarch, milk, egg, baking powder and seasonings to make a thin batter. Pour the pineapple and its syrup into a saucepan, stir in the sugar and heat very gently and thoroughly.

Pour canola oil into a heavy skillet to a depth of 2-1/2". Heat to 375° on a deep-fat frying thermometer.

When ready, drain the fish of extra soy sauce, dip quickly into the batter, drain a bit, and plunge into the hot oil. Add as many pieces as you can at one time, but be sure that the temperature of the oil stays at 375°. The fish will cook in about 1 or 2 minutes. The crust will be crisp, feathery and golden. Remove to a pan lined with paper towels and keep in a warm oven until all the fish is ready.

Mix 1 Tbsp. of cornstarch with 1/4 cup water, add to heating pineapple and cook until syrup has thickened. Arrange the pineapple and sauce on a warm serving platter.

Place the fish pieces carefully on top. Makes 6 servings.

COLD POACHED SALMON

Perfect for a summer buffet. Fill pastry bag with mayonnaise. Use a star tip to decorate salmon. This dish can be prepared well ahead of time.

Court Bouillon:

2 cups dry white wine

1 quart of water

4 sprigs of parsley

1 onion, sliced

2 slices of lemon

1 tsp. salt

3 cloves

6 peppercorns

1 bay leaf

1/2 salmon, filleted

Cucumber Dill Sauce:

1 cup of sour cream

1 Tbsp. minced dill

1/2 cup cucumber, peeled and chopped

1 tsp. minced chives

Place all ingredients in a fish poacher and bring to boil. Lower heat and simmer for 30 minutes.

Wrap salmon fillet in cheesecloth or lay on fish poacher insert. Lower fish into bouillon and return to boil. Turn heat down to simmer only. Remember the broth barely moves. Allow 7 minutes to the pound, then let fish cool in the broth. This also finishes the cooking.

When done, lift fish out of the water, peel off the skin and gently roll onto a platter. Remove cheesecloth, if used. Chill salmon and serve with cucumber dill sauce.

For the dill sauce, combine the ingredients listed to the left.

Cousins

Barbara, Judy and Maddy

Vivien and Chip

Marcia and Marc

Seymour Grubman

BEEF & LAMB

BEEF STROGANOFF

Recipe from Grandma Blanche

2 lbs. Sirloin steak, cut into 1/2 inch cubes

3 Tbsp. canola oil

1 large onion, chopped

1 clove garlic, chopped

2 Tbsp. flour

1 3-oz. can (3/4 cup) browned mushrooms and broth

1/2 cup chopped celery

1 8-oz. can tomato sauce

2 tsp. salt

1/8 tsp. pepper

1 tsp. Worcestershire sauce

1 cup sour cream

Brown steak cubes in oil. Add onion and garlic. Cook until golden. Stir in flour.

Add all remaining ingredients except sour cream. Mix well.

Turn into greased 3 quart casserole.

Bake uncovered in moderate oven (325°) until meat is tender, about 1-1/2 hours.

Slowly stir in sour cream, and serve.

SHORT RIBS

Recipe from Grandma Blanche

short ribs

canola oil

onion

fresh basil

garlic powder

salt and pepper

dried celery leaves

1 can tomato sauce

1 can chopped tomatoes

1/2 cup water

Cut all visible fat off short ribs. Brown in small amount of canola oil. Pour off oil.

Add diced onions, fresh basil, garlic powder, salt & pepper, dried celery leaves, 1 can tomato sauce, 1 can chopped tomatoes, 1/2 cup water.

Cover and cook in 350° oven for approximately 2 hours, or until tender.

Hobo Steak

The maitre d' at a Hollywood hotspot gave me this recipe. My brother's 21st birthday was held there. The place has since closed, but this recipe lives on. Despite the name, this steak should not be eaten in a boxcar while on the run.

2 double New York steaks,
cut 2" thick

freshly ground black pepper

salt

sourdough French bread

1/4 lb. unsalted butter

Preheat broiler.

Trim the fat from the steaks and set aside. Season steaks with freshly ground black pepper. Flatten the trimmed fat and form it around the outside of the steaks. Tie with string. This protects the steaks from shrinking as well as keeping the juices in and the meat moist.

Prepare a salt pack. Mix salt and water into a mush. Apply the salt pack in a 2" mound on the steaks. (The salt does not penetrate the meat or make it salty.) Broil for about 10 minutes. Carefully remove the salt pack, turn the steaks, replace the salt on the other side. Broil for 10 minutes more.

Slice the sourdough French bread about 1/2" thick and toast.

Heat butter in frying pan until bubbling.

Remove the salt crust from the steak. Cut away the fat and string, and slice on the bias. Place the steak slices in the foaming butter, and cook to desired doneness, about 1 minute on each side.

Remove meat from butter and place on the toast. Spoon some hot butter over each piece.

Serve immediately.

BRISKET

Recipe from Grandma Blanche

1 brisket–about 2-1/2 lbs.

3 celery stalks

4 carrots

1 onion, chopped

1 bay leaf

salt, pepper, paprika, garlic to season

Cut fat from brisket and brown on each side.

Cut onion, celery and carrot and put into pot.

Add 2 to 3 cups of water to half-cover the meat.

Add seasoning after meat has cooked 45 minutes.

After 2 hours, pierce it to see if it is tender.

Remove brisket from pot. Pour liquid and vegetables into a strainer and puree them.

Taste. Add more salt if necessary.

Let meat cool, then cover and refrigerate. Refrigerate sauce separately.

The next day remove the fat layer from the sauce.

Slice meat and cover with sauce. Heat and enjoy.

BRISKET #2

Recipe from Grandma Blanche

1 brisket–about 2-1/2 lbs.
Grey Poupon mustard
onion soup mix
1/2 cup water

Trim all fat from brisket. Brush with Grey Poupon mustard.

Place meat in heavy foil.

Cover meat with one package of onion soup mix and 1/2 cup water.

Roll brisket in mixture until covered on all sides.

Close foil tight and place in baking pan.

Bake 5 hours in 250° oven. When cooled, unwrap. Place brisket on dish and refrigerate overnight.

Put gravy in separate bowl and refrigerate.

The following day slice brisket and remove fat from gravy. Heat and serve.

FILET OF BEEF
WITH STRAWBERRY VINEGAR SAUCE

Recipe from Lynn and Carl Hanauer

This is one of my favorite recipes.

Strawberry Marinade:

1 cup Strawberry vinegar

1 medium onion, finely chopped

1 medium carrot, finely chopped

2 Tbsp. olive oil

2 bay leaves

2 5" long marjoram branches

1 small garlic clove, sliced

6 to 8 cracked peppercorns

1 2-lb. beef tenderloin, trimmed

Strawberry Sauce:

2 Tbsp. olive oil or butter

2 Tbsp. onion, finely chopped

2 Tbsp. leek, white part only, finely chopped

1 Tbsp. carrot, finely chopped

2 cups rich beef or veal stock

2 Tbsp. red currant jelly or strawberry jam

For Marinade:

Combine vinegar, onion, carrot, oil, bay leaves, marjoram, garlic and peppercorns in medium saucepan and bring to boil over high heat. Cool. Set tenderloin in baking dish.

Cover with marinade. Refrigerate overnight.

For Sauce:

Strain marinade. Reserve. Heat oil in heavy medium saucepan over low heat.

Add onion, leek and carrot and cook until lightly browned, about 7 minutes.

Add stock, increase heat and bring to boil.

Reduce heat and simmer until reduced to about 1-3/4 cups.

Blend in jelly or jam, salt, pepper and 3/4 cup strained marinade. Simmer 20 minutes.

Strain. Sauce should measure about 1-1/2 cups. Set aside.

Preheat oven to 450°.

Strawberry Sauce (continued)

1 tsp. salt

freshly ground pepper

2 Tbsp. butter

1 Tbsp. olive oil

salt and freshly ground pepper

1 cup fresh chopped strawberries

Heat 1 Tbsp. butter with remaining oil in ovenproof heavy large skillet over high heat. Pat tenderloin dry.

Brown well on all sides and ends. Remove from heat. Season with salt and pepper.

Roast until cooked to desired doneness. Remove tenderloin from skillet.

Pour sauce into same skillet.

Place over high heat and boil until thickened, scraping up any browned bits.

Remove from heat and swirl in remaining 1 Tbsp. of butter. Stir in strawberries. Spoon some sauce onto heated platter.

Slice tenderloin and arrange on platter.

Spoon remaining sauce over and serve.
Makes 6 to 8 servings.

FILET OF BEEF WELLINGTON

Recipe from Andrea Bernard

I've made this many times. The 2-page recipe looks like a lot of work, but it's really quite manageable, and definitely worth the time and effort. Not only is the finished product delicious, it's a work of art.

4 lb. filet of beef, trimmed of all fat and trussed for roasting

1/4 cup olive oil (not extra virgin)

2 cups onion, coarsely chopped (2 large)

1 cup sliced celery

1/2 cup dry sherry or Madeira

2 (10-oz.) cans beef broth

1 Tbsp. cornstarch

1 Tbsp. water

1/4 cup minced shallots

1/4 cup butter

1 lb. mushrooms, very finely diced

1/2 tsp. salt

dash of pepper

pastry for 2 crust pie *(I use Pillsbury Refrigerated Crescent Dough)*

1 egg yolk

1 Tbsp. water

Brown the filet. Heat the oil in a roasting pan over medium heat, add the filet, brown it on all sides. Remove the filet and set it aside to cool for one hour. Add the onions and celery to the fat remaining in the roasting pan, sauté until the onions are translucent.

Pour off the fat in the pan, add the sherry or madeira (avert your face). Cook for 1 minute. Add the beef broth and bring to a boil. Blend the cornstarch with 1 Tbsp. of water, stir it into the mixture in the pan and continue stirring until the sauce has thickened. Simmer sauce for 10 to 15 minutes and correct the seasoning. Strain sauce and set aside until ready to heat and serve.

Make the filling. Cook the shallots 2 minutes in butter in a large skillet over medium heat. Add the mushrooms, salt and pepper, and cook 7 to 8 minutes, or until all the moisture disappears, stirring occasionally. Turn the mixture into a bowl. Taste and correct seasoning if needed. Cool.

The crust. Prepare the pastry. Turn it out on a lightly floured surface and roll it out with a lightly floured rolling pin to a rectangle 3 to 4" longer than the filet and wide enough to encase the filet.

Assemble the Wellington. Spoon about a third of the mushroom mixture down the center of the pastry rectangle. Un-truss the filet and place it over the mushroom mixture. Spoon the rest of the mixture onto the filet, patting it in place if necessary.

To encase the filet, bring one side of the pastry up and over the filet, then lift and bring the opposite side up and over. Moisten the long edge and press it firmly to seal it.

Moisten the ends. Tuck them in and press to seal firmly.

Place the wrapped filet on ungreased cookie sheet, seam side down.

To let the steam escape during baking, make a small hole in each end and two or three on the top. Cut designs from the pastry scraps (i.e. leaves with a pastry wheel). Moisten them and place them on the filet.

You may cover the filet with aluminum foil and refrigerate it overnight. If you do, let it stand at room temperature for 30 minutes before baking.

Just before baking, beat the egg yolk with 1 tablespoon of water and brush it over the pastry.

Bake at 425° for 30 minutes. Remove it from the cookie sheet carefully with 2 broad spatulas and place it on a serving platter. Let it stand for 20 minutes before slicing. Slice the Wellington and serve with heated wine sauce. Makes 6 to 8 servings.

I have never made this recipe using a whole filet. I have always prepared individual beef Wellingtons. I like to decorate each individual pastry with my guest's initials surrounded by leaves.

Andrea and I have always had lots of fun together.

Viennese Goulash

Recipe from Tess Braun

Steven's and Carrie's grandparents, Tess and Fred Braun, were from Vienna. There was always something good cooking in Tess's kitchen.

2 tsp. marjoram, crushed

1 tsp. finely chopped lemon rind

1 garlic clove, crushed

3/4 cup butter

1 tsp. tomato paste

2 lbs. onions, sliced

1 Tbsp. sweet Hungarian paprika

2 lbs. beef cut into uniform chunks

1 cup water (more may be needed as the goulash cooks)

1/4 cup flour

salt and pepper, to taste

Melt butter in a large pot. Add marjoram, lemon rind, garlic and tomato paste. Stir.

Add onions and sauté the mixture, stirring constantly, until onions are golden.

Add the sweet Hungarian paprika and cook the onions, stirring constantly for another 1/2 minute.

Add the beef, 1 cup of water and salt and pepper to taste.

Cover tightly, and simmer until beef is tender, about 1-1/2 hours. Add a little more water during cooking if necessary.

Just before the goulash is done, add 1/2 cup water and let the sauce boil up once more. If more sauce is desired, sprinkle it with 1/4 cup flour just before the water is added at the end and add 1 more cup of water.

Serve the goulash with Spatzle, noodles, or boiled potatoes.

Fred and Tess

Osso Bucco

Recipe from Cristiana Schneider

4-5 thick veal shanks
flour
1 onion, chopped
olive oil or butter
1 cup white wine
3 large tomatoes, diced
1 cup beef stock
1 celery stalk, finely diced
1 carrot, finely chopped
salt and pepper to taste
parsley for garnish

Dust the veal with flour. In a large pan, brown veal on both sides in olive oil or butter. Set aside.

Add onion, celery, and carrot to the pan and sauté for a few minutes.

Return meat to pan. Add salt, pepper, and wine.

Cook for 2 minutes and add the stock. Lower the heat.

Cover and cook for 40 minutes. Add tomatoes, and more stock if needed, and cook until meat is tender.

Add chopped parsley, if desired and cook 2 more minutes.

Judy and Cristiana

STUFFED CABBAGE

Recipe from Grandma Blanche

1 large cabbage

Meat Mixture:

2 lbs. ground beef

1 carrot, shredded

1 onion, chopped small

2 eggs

1 cup corn flake crumbs

handful oatmeal

1/4 cup water

salt and pepper

Sauce:

1 Tbsp. butter

1 onion, chopped

1 small can tomato sauce

2 small cans tomato soup

1 cup brown sugar

1/2 cup lemon juice

1 bay leaf

Remove core from large cabbage. Boil whole cabbage, core side down, in approximately 2" of water for 10 to 15 minutes.

Remove outer leaves that are tender, and put the rest of the head back in the pot and boil until tender (5 to 7 minutes). Trim heavy stem of each leaf. It makes it easier to roll.

Prepare meat mixture.

Starting at the stem end of the leaf, roll 2 to 3 Tbsp. of meat into cabbage leaf. As you roll, tuck in the sides of the leaf to make a neat package. Make extra meat into meatballs.

Chop extra cabbage leaves that are too small to roll.

In a large pot melt 1 Tbsp. butter. Sauté one small onion (chopped) for 5 minutes until limp. Add chopped cabbage and sauté for 2 to 3 minutes more. Add salt to taste. Place cabbage rolls on top of cabbage/onion mixture. Place meatballs on top of cabbage rolls. Pour the following over contents of pot, in this order: tomato sauce, tomato soup, brown sugar, lemon juice, and bay leaf.

Cook on top of stove covered for 1 hour, over a small flame. Add lemon juice or brown sugar to taste. Heat oven to 350°. Place uncovered pot in the oven. Cook for 1 to 1-1/2 hours uncovered, or until brown.

LAMB SHANKS

Recipe from Grandma Blanche

6 lamb shanks
1 stalk celery, chopped
1 onion, chopped
1 bay leaf
Lawrey's seasoned salt
garlic salt
4 Tbsp. currant jelly
3 Tbsp. chili sauce

Cut all fat off 6 lamb shanks. In a large pot, sear shanks on all sides until brown, then add enough water to just cover them.

Add the celery, onion, bay leaf, seasoned salt, and garlic salt to the pot.

Start on high heat until it boils. For the first few minutes of cooking remove all the scum that accumulates on top of water. Repeat after 15 minutes.

Simmer, covered over medium heat until tender, approx. 1 hour.

Remove when tender and place in shallow dish.

Dissolve 4 Tbsp. currant jelly over low heat.

Add 3 Tbsp. chili sauce. Brush over lamb, turn and brush other side.

Pour extra sauce over lamb. Bake at 300° for 30 to 45 minutes, until brown. Baste lamb with sauce while it is baking.

I always double the sauce recipe because it's so good.

LAMB SHANKS #2

Recipe from Grandma Blanche's friend, Sadell Deman

6 lamb shanks

1 large onion, chopped

1-1/2 cups catsup

8 tsp. Lea & Perrins Worcestershire Sauce

4-5 tsp. sugar

2 tsp. Colman's dry mustard

2 tsp. paprika

1 tsp. Tabasco sauce

1/2 cup vinegar

2 garlic cloves, chopped

1-1/2 cups water

Brown lamb shanks on all sides. Transfer to an ovenproof pan. In a separate pan, brown 1 large onion, chopped.

Add the catsup, Worcestershire Sauce, sugar, dry mustard, paprika, Tabasco sauce, vinegar, chopped garlic cloves, and water.

Pour mixture over lamb shanks.

Cover pot.

Bake at 350° for about 2 hours or until tender.

Our home in Starwood
Aspen, Colorado

VEGETABLES

BAKED SUMMER SQUASH

Recipe from Grandma Blanche

2 lbs. summer squash
3 eggs, beaten
melted butter
1 cup matzo meal
1/2 cup grated onion

Cook the squash. Drain and mash well.

Add eggs, a little melted butter, matzo meal and grated onion.

Mix well. Pour into greased square pan or greased muffin pans.

Bake at 375° for 1 hour.

Grandma Blanche (about 16-years-old here) was a pianist in a music shop owned by Irving Berlin. People would pick out sheet music, and she would play it so they could decide if they wanted to buy it.

Judy's Baked Fennel
with Parmesan Cheese

fennel bulbs 1/4″
to 1/2″ thick

butter or oilive oil

Parmesan cheese

salt and pepper

Slice several fennel bulbs 1/4″ to 1/2″ thick.

Boil for 5 to 7 minutes.

Drain fennel and lay in baking dish.

Top with butter or olive oil.

Sprinkle with Parmesan cheese, salt and pepper.

Bake at 350° for 20 minutes.

Backstage at the MUNY. In 2006, I worked as a production assistant on Breakfast at Tiffany's.

CARROT RING

Recipe from Arlene Grubman

1 cup of shortening

1/2 cup brown sugar

1 egg, slightly beaten

1 tsp. cold water

2 cups grated carrots (grate on large grater)

1-1/2 cups flour, sifted

1/2 tsp. baking soda

1 tsp. baking powder

1/2 tsp. nutmeg (optional)

1/2 tsp. salt

1 tsp. cinnamon

Preheat oven to 350°.

Cream the shortening and brown sugar.

Beat in egg, water, flour, cinnamon, baking powder, baking soda, nutmeg, and salt until blended.

Stir in carrots. Pour into greased 6 cup ring mold.

Bake 30 minutes or until done.

Unmold and serve.

This recipe can be made in advance and refrigerated. Remove from refrigerator 30 minutes before baking.

My mother and father, Arlene and Seymour Grubman

STUFFED EGGPLANTS

6 firm eggplants

1 large bunch of fresh parsley,
finely minced

2-4 cloves of fresh garlic, finely
chopped

1 cup bread crumbs

3/4 cup olive oil

salt and pepper

Preheat the oven to 450°.

Cut eggplants in two, lengthwise, without peeling
them. With a teaspoon, scoop out as much flesh as
possible. Reserve it.

Place the eggplant shells, flesh side up, in a
roasting pan.

Sauté the reserved flesh in a little olive oil with salt
and pepper.

Make a stuffing of the finely minced parsley,
chopped garlic, cooked flesh of the eggplants, the
bread crumbs and pepper.

Fill the eggplant shells with the mixture.

Add a dot of butter on each one. Pour the
remaining olive oil generously over them.

Lower to 250° and cook for approximately one
hour. This dish is a perfect garnish for all grilled or
roasted meats. Makes 6 servings.

*To save time, rather than stuffing the eggplants, I
sometimes just cut the eggplant into cubes and combine with
the remaining ingredients. Bake in a casserole dish.*

Judy's Creamed Carrots

This recipe is delicious. I have been making it since my children were babies.

2-1/2 lbs. carrots

1 qt. chicken broth

2 stalks celery, sliced

2 heads shallots, chopped coarsely

1 tsp. salt

1/4 tsp. white pepper

1 bay leaf

4 Tbsp. butter

1 tsp. minced shallots

Cream Sauce:

4 Tbsp. butter

4 Tbsp. flour

2 cups heavy cream*

salt and pepper

Place peeled and cut carrots into pot with chicken broth, celery, chopped shallots, salt, pepper and bay leaf.

Bring to boil, reduce heat, cover and cook 20 minutes or until carrots are tender. Drain, reserving stock for other use. Discard bay leaf.

Place carrots and vegetables through coarse grinder or mash with potato masher. Melt 2 Tbsp. butter until browned.

Add shallots and cook 1 minute. Add ground carrot mixture, cook and stir over very low heat until water has evaporated.

Mix with cream sauce. Bring to boil and stir in remaining 2 Tbsp. of butter until melted. Makes 6 to 8 servings.

Cream Sauce:
Melt butter and stir in flour until smooth. Gradually add heavy cream*.

Cook and stir until smooth and slightly thickened. Season to taste with salt and pepper.

* Sometimes I use whole milk instead of cream.

This photo was taken at our home in Starwood, Aspen.

Pickled Beets

Recipe from Marilyn Gilbert

beets (small)
2 cups sugar
2 cups water
2 cups cider vinegar
1 tsp. cloves
1 tsp. allspice
1 Tbsp. cinnamon

Select small beets. Cook until tender, testing them with a fork. Dip in cold water and peel.

Mix together the sugar, water, cider vinegar, cloves, allspice, and cinnamon to make the syrup.

Mix all of the above and poor over the beets.

Boil for 10 minutes.

Pack into sterilized canning jars and seal at once.

To sterilize jars: boil rubberized tops. Wash glass jars in dishwasher.

Marilyn is amazing. . . she is a lawyer, an opera singer, and she can cook!

Parsnip & Pear Puree

Recipe from Gaylene Ray

6 cups coarsely peeled and chopped parsnips

1/2 stick of butter

2 d'Anjou pears, peeled and chopped

1 Tbsp. Cognac

1/2 cup crème fraîche or sour cream

1/4 tsp. allspice

salt and pepper to taste

Cook parsnips in water, covered, for 20 minutes. Drain.

Melt butter in a small skillet over medium heat, add pears and cook for 5 minutes.

Add cognac, and continue to cook for 15 minutes, stirring constantly.

Put all ingredients in food processor. (Can be prepared a day ahead to this point.) Add creme fraiche or sour cream, allspice and salt and pepper.

I use 3 pears and 2 tablespoons of cognac, and a little more butter.

Gaylene keeps Billy and Patty on their toes!

Southern Cooked Greens

Wes's mother's family was from Atlanta, Georgia, and they all loved traditional southern cooking.

3-4 strips chopped bacon

3 cups chopped onions

salt to taste

freshly ground pepper to taste

1/2 cup firmly packed light brown sugar

2 Tbsp. minced shallots

1 Tbsp. minced garlic

6 cups water

1/4 cup rice wine vinegar

6 lbs. collard greens (you can substitute mustard greens, turnip greens, kale or spinach) washed and stemmed

Sauté the bacon in a large pot, until slightly crisp. Add the onions, salt and pepper.

Cook 6 to 7 minutes, until the onions are translucent.

Add the brown sugar and stir to dissolve. Add shallots and garlic. Cook for 2 minutes.

Add the water and vinegar and mix well.

Begin adding the greens, a third at a time, pressing them down as they begin to wilt. Season with salt and pepper.

Reduce heat to medium-low and cook, uncovered, until the greens are soft, about 1-1/4 hour.

Judy and Wes

Pearl Onions

pearl onions

strawberry vinegar

sugar

Cook pearl onions in strawberry vinegar and sugar until done.

My handsome husband!

STUFFED ZUCCHINI

Recipe from Billy

4 to 5 zucchini

1 egg

1 finely chopped onion

1 to 2 cups grated cheddar cheese

1 cup (about) of bread crumbs

butter

Slice 4 to 5 zucchini in half lengthwise. With a knife, make slits on inside of zucchini (not all the way through) so it will cook faster than the outside.

Boil 4 to 5 minutes, until inside is soft but green shell is still firm.

Drain and cool. Remove inside of zucchini to a bowl, and mix with 1 egg, 1 finely chopped onion, 1 to 2 cups grated cheddar cheese and about 1 cup of bread crumbs.

Stuff zucchini halves with mixture.

Sprinkle bread crumbs on top.

Drizzle with a little melted butter. (Can be made ahead to this point.)

Bake at 350° until cheese melts and tops are brown.

Patty, Judy and Billy

Billy at his Thanksgiving table.

COWBOY BEANS

Recipe from Lou Nelson

A classic camping recipe from author and writing mentor, Lou Nelson.

4 strips of bacon, crisply fried and crumbled (reserve 2-3 Tbsp. drippings)

1/2 cup onion, finely diced

1/2 cup diced bell pepper (optional)

16 oz. can Bush's homestyle baked beans

16 oz. can pork-and-beans

2-3 Tbsp. molasses

1/3 cup catsup

1/2 tsp. Coleman's dry mustard

ground black pepper to taste

Sauté onions and bell pepper in bacon drippings till soft.

Add both cans of beans, the molasses, dry mustard, catsup, bacon bits, and pepper to taste.

Simmer for a few minutes to mix flavors.

Pour into greased casserole dish and bake at 350° for 30 minutes until bubbly. Cool slightly and serve.

Lou

POTATOES AND SWEET POTATOES

Mom's Potato Salad

Russet potatoes, boiled,
peeled and sliced

hard boiled eggs

diced celery

mayonnaise

salt and pepper

Mix potatoes, hard boiled eggs, and diced celery together.

Mix with mayonnaise.

Add salt and pepper to taste.

You can add dill if you like.

My Mom, Arlene

Potato Pancakes or Potato Pudding

5 large potatoes, grated	Stir and mix well. Fry in canola oil.
1 onion, grated	To make a pudding, use the same ingredients:
2 tsp. baking powder	Add 1 stick melted butter to the ingredients. Stir and mix well.
3 slices of white bread, soaked in milk	Poor into greased ovenproof casserole. Cover.
5 eggs	Cook for one hour. Uncover, cook until done. 350° oven.

OVEN CRISP POTATOES

Recipe from Mom

potatoes
butter
salt
paprika

Preheat oven to 450°. Peel potatoes and slice thick.

Lay only 1 layer in baking pan and dot with butter.

Add salt and paprika.

Bring water to a boil on top of stove. Add enough water to the pan to cover potatoes 3/4 of the way up.

Top of potato should not be under water.

Bake in lower part of oven for 1 hour, then turn potatoes over and bake another 1/2 hour.

Arlene on the Orient Express

Arlene

POTATO PANCAKES

Recipe from Nanny Tess

eggs
white or red rose potatoes
salt and pepper
matzo meal
onion powder (optional)
canola oil

Use 1 egg for each large potato. Use white or red rose potatoes.

Grate potatoes finely. Mix with eggs.

Add salt, pepper and matzo meal to give it body. You can use some onion powder too.

Drop by wooden spoonfuls into hot canola oil.

Make them thin. Turn them only once.

Don't use too much oil. Keep adding oil as more pancakes are cooked.

SWEET POTATO CASSEROLE

I have made this many times at Thanksgiving. Everyone loves this recipe.

1-1/2 lb. sweet potatoes
1/2 cup granulated sugar
1/2 cup milk
1 egg, beaten
3 Tbsp. butter, cubed
1 tsp. vanilla
1/2 cup packed brown sugar
1/3 cup all-purpose flour
2 Tbsp. butter
1/2 cup pecan pieces
pecan halves (optional)

Peel sweet potatoes, and cut into cubes. Cook, covered, in a small amount of boiling water for about 30 minutes or until tender. Drain.

Combine hot sweet potatoes, granulated sugar, milk, egg, the 3 Tbsp. butter and vanilla. With a wooden spoon, stir to break up potatoes but not completely mash them.

Put mixture into a greased 2-quart square baking dish.

Combine brown sugar and flour; cut in 2 Tbsp. butter until mixture resembles coarse crumbs.

Stir in pecan pieces and sprinkle crumb mixture on top of potatoes.

Bake, uncovered, in a 350° oven about 25 minutes or till set.

Garnish with pecan halves, if desired.
Makes 8 servings as a side dish.

BOURBON-WALNUT YAMS

Every Thanksgiving, my friends request this recipe.

4 pounds red-skinned yams
1/2 cup whipping cream
6 Tbsp. butter
1/3 cup pure maple syrup
3 Tbsp. bourbon
1-1/2 tsp. ground cinnamon
1 tsp. ground allspice
3/4 tsp. ground nutmeg
1 cup chopped walnuts

Preheat oven to 350°. Roast yams on rimmed baking sheet until tender, about 1 hour.

Cool slightly. Scoop inside of yams into large bowl. Discard skins.

Mash yams into coarse puree.

Stir cream and butter into hot yams.

Stir in syrup, bourbon and all spices.

Season with salt and pepper. Sprinkle nuts over and serve.

DO AHEAD. Can be prepared 1 day ahead.

Cover and chill. Re-warm in microwave.

Sprinkle nuts over and serve.

GOLDEN POTATO CASSEROLE

Recipe from Mom

6 medium potatoes

2 cups sour cream

10 oz. sharp cheddar cheese, shredded

1 bunch green onions, chopped

3 Tbsp. milk

1 tsp. salt

1/8 tsp. pepper

2 Tbsp. melted butter

1/3 cup bread crumbs

Cook potatoes in boiling water until tender. Remove, cool and peel.

Grate, using a coarse grater. Add sour cream, cheese, onions, milk, salt and pepper. Mix thoroughly.

Turn into greased 9" x 13" pan.

Smooth top with spatula.

Combine melted butter and bread crumbs and sprinkle over top.

Bake at 350° for 50 minutes or until piping hot.

Cut into squares and serve. Makes 8 servings.

Arlene and Judy

PASTA, COUSCOUS, RICE & RISOTTO

TRADITIONAL NOODLE PUDDING

Recipe from Grandma Blanche

8 oz. noodles, cooked

3 eggs, separated

1/2 cup golden raisins

1 apple, grated

1/4 tsp. salt

1/2 cup sugar

1/2 tsp. cinnamon

4 Tbsp. melted butter

Beat egg whites stiff.

To hot noodles, add beaten egg yolks, golden raisins, grated apple, sugar, salt, cinnamon, and melted butter. Mix well. Fold in beaten egg whites.

Pour into a greased pan. Bake at 350° for 1 hour.

My Grandpa, Sam Fiedler, was first violinist in the MGM Studio Orchestra

NOODLE PUDDING

Recipe from Grandma Blanche

8 oz. broad noodles, cooked

4 eggs, beaten

3 cups milk

1 large 16-oz. carton cottage cheese

1 large 16-oz. carton sour cream

6 Tbsp. sugar

1 cup corn flake crumbs

3 Tbsp. melted butter

cinnamon

Combine noodles, eggs, milk, cottage cheese, sour cream and sugar. Mix well.

Pour into a 9" x 10" pan.

Combine corn flake crumbs and melted butter. Spread on top. Sprinkle with a little cinnamon.

Bake at 350° for 45 minutes.

Our home was across the street from a dichondra farm. That farm is now the 101 Freeway.

GENOVESE BASIL PESTO

Recipe from author and editor Laura Taylor

2 cups basil
1 cup parsley
6 garlic cloves
1/2 - 3/4 cup olive oil
1/2 cup toasted pine nuts
1/4 cup Parmesan, grated
salt and pepper to taste

Use food processor to blend first 3 ingredients.

Add remaining ingredients to desired consistency.

Can be frozen.

Laura's family has occupied the same house in Tuscany for over 750 years. This recipe is from her village, Coreglia.

MEAT SAUCE, BOLOGNESE STYLE

Recipe from Mark Bennett

I once walked into Mark's house while this sauce was simmering on the stove. The fragrance was delectable!

3 Tbsp. chopped onion

3 Tbsp. olive oil

3 Tbsp. butter

3 Tbsp. chopped celery

3 Tbsp. chopped carrot

3/4 lb. ground lean beef

salt

1 cup dry white wine

1/2 cup milk

1/8 tsp. nutmeg

2 cups canned Italian tomatoes, roughly chopped with their juice

In a deep, heavy, enameled, cast-iron pot—to keep the ragu from reducing too quickly— heat the oil and butter over medium heat.

Add the chopped onion and sauté briefly until just translucent.

Add the celery and carrot and cook for 2 minutes.

Keeping medium heat, add the ground beef, crumbling it in the pot with a fork.

Add 1/2 tsp. salt, stir, and cook just until the meat has lost its raw red color (it must NOT brown or it will lose delicacy).

Add the wine, turn up the heat to medium high, and cook, stirring occasionally until all the wine has evaporated.

Turn the heat down to medium, add the milk and nutmeg, cook until the milk has evaporated. Stir frequently. When the milk has evaporated, add the tomatoes and stir thoroughly.

When mixture starts to bubble, turn the heat down until the sauce cooks at the tiniest simmer, just an occasional bubble.

Cook, uncovered, for a minimum of 3-1/2 to 4 hours, stirring occasionally. (Cooking up to 5 hours is best, as the flavor increases as it cooks.)

Taste and correct for salt.

If you cannot watch the sauce for such a long stretch, you can turn off the heat and resume cooking it later on. But do finish cooking it in one day.

Ragu can be kept in the refrigerator for up to 5 days, or frozen. Reheat until it simmers for about 15 minutes before using.

Serve with tagliatelle, tortellini, lasagne, rigatoni, ziti, conchiglie or rotelle pasta. Makes 6 servings, about 2-1/4 cups.

Mark

Homemade Ricotta Cheese

It's very important to make sure the pot and utensils are cleaned properly. This is really easy to make, and tastes delicious over pasta with a little tomato sauce.

1 gallon whole milk

1 cup heavy cream

1/2 cup freshly squeezed lemon juice

salt, optional

Prepare sanitizing solution: 1 quart of water plus 1 tablespoon of household bleach.

Rinse a large stainless steel pot with the sanitizing solution, then pour the milk and cream into the pot.

Place over medium-high heat and bring to a boil. Stir with a sanitized spoon. Don't let the milk become scorched on the bottom of the pot. Reduce heat to low and stir in the lemon juice.

Stir slowly until the milk curdles and white curds float to the top. Remove pot from heat and cover. In about 5 minutes the curds will become firmer.

Rinse a colander and several layers of cheesecloth in the sanitizing solution. Wring excess water from cheesecloth.

Line the colander with the cloth, and set it in the sink or over a large bowl.

With a sanitized perforated spoon, gently ladle the curds into the colander.

Let the whey drain for 30 minutes, or until the ricotta is still moist but fairly dry.

After 15 minutes, lift the edges of the cloth toward the center of the colander to loosen the cheese from the cloth. This will facilitate draining.

After 30 minutes, if the texture of the ricotta is still too runny, gather the edges of the cloth together, wrap with a piece of kitchen string to make a bag, and tie it closed.

Hang the bag containing the ricotta cheese from the faucet or the handle of a kitchen cabinet door so the excess whey can drip from the bag into the sink or a bowl.

If adding salt, place the ricotta into a sanitized bowl and stir in the salt.

Place ricotta in an airtight container and store in the refrigerator.

Use within 5 days. Makes about 3 cups.

COLD SESAME NOODLES

1/2 pound linguine, or other pasta, cooked and cooled

1 cucumber, peeled, seeded and diced

1 bunch scallions, sliced thin, including most of the green

1 cup bean sprouts

1 carrot, shredded

1 cup snow peas

1/2 cup chopped fresh cilantro

1/4 cup toasted sesame seeds

Cold Sesame Noodle Dressing:

2 scallions, chopped, including green

1/3 cup chicken broth

1/4 cup smooth peanut butter, sugar free

1/4 cup cider vinegar or rice wine vinegar

1/4 cup low sodium soy sauce

2 tsp. dark sesame oil

Place drained noodles into a large bowl.

Blend all the dressing ingredients in a blender or food processor and pour over noodles. Mix thoroughly.

Add remaining ingredients, mix well and serve. Or you can cover and chill noodles combined with dressing, then mix in the vegetables right before serving.

Makes 6 servings.

Couscous Salad—The Best Ever!

This is truly an all-time favorite. It can be made well in advance.

2/3 cup dried currants

3 Tbsp. unsalted butter

1/8 tsp. powdered saffron

1-1/2 cups chicken stock

1-1/2 cups couscous

1-1/2 cups diced celery

1/3 cup green onion, sliced thin

1/3 cup pine nuts

1/4 cup fresh parsley, minced

1/4 cup fresh lemon juice

1/4 tsp. ground cinnamon

1/2 cup olive oil

salt and pepper

Soak currants in enough water to cover them for 15 minutes, then drain and set aside.

In large skillet, melt butter and stir in saffron over medium heat.

Add stock and bring to boil. Stir in couscous, cover and remove from heat. Let mixture stand 4 minutes.

Transfer couscous to a large bowl, breaking up any lumps with a fork.

Add celery, currants, green onions, pine nuts and parsley. Mix well.

In small bowl, whisk together lemon juice and cinnamon.

Add olive oil in slow, steady stream, whisking constantly until emulsified. Drizzle dressing over salad and toss.

Season to taste with salt and pepper.

Makes 6 servings.

* May be made 1 day ahead and stored, covered in refrigerator until ready to use.

SMOKED SALMON PASTA

2 tsp. butter

2 tsp. shallots, chopped

1 clove garlic, chopped

3 or 4 oz. smoked salmon, chopped (lox)

2 oz. vodka

1/2 cup whipping cream

1/4 cup clam juice

1 Tbsp. tomato paste

1/2 cup frozen peas

salt and pepper to taste

penne or rigatoni, cooked according to package directions

Sauté shallots in melted butter for 1 minute.

Add chopped garlic, sauté for 1 to 2 minutes more.

Add the smoked salmon, sauté for 1 minute. Make sure to separate the salmon pieces.

Add the vodka, either off the heat or on very low heat, as it may flame up.

Add the cream, clam juice, tomato paste, and peas.

Bring to a boil, then turn heat to low and simmer for 5 minutes.

Add salt and pepper to taste. Add cooked pasta to pan and stir.

Low-Calorie Vegetable Lasagne

My friends love this dish.

1/2 pound dried lasagne noodles

1 pound carrots

1 pound zucchini

1 cup part skim ricotta cheese

2 Tbsp. chopped fresh basil

2 tsp. chopped fresh oregano

1/2 tsp. fresh ground pepper

12 ounces frozen spinach

4 cups marinara sauce

1-1/2 cups shredded part skim mozzarella

Cook lasagne noodles according to package directions until tender. Drain. Place noodles in cold water until ready to use.

Preheat oven to 375°.

With mandolin or kitchen slicer at thinnest setting, cut carrots and zucchini lengthwise into paper-thin strips.

Mix ricotta, basil, oregano, 1/4 tsp. salt and the pepper in small bowl.

Layer 1/3 of the noodles on the bottom of 9" x 13" glass baking dish. Trim noodles if necessary.

Layer half the spinach, then half the carrots and zucchini. Top with half the ricotta mixture.

Repeat, layering another third of the noodles and remaining vegetables and cheese.

Top with noodles. Cover with foil. Bake 35 minutes, until vegetables are tender.

Preheat broiler. Cut lasagne into 6 squares, and top with 3 cups marinara sauce.

Spread mozzarella on top. Broil 2 minutes. Pass remaining sauce.

Makes 6 servings.

Sun Dried Tomato Risotto

Recipe from Wes's sister Robin Whitmore

8-10 sun dried tomatoes (not packed in oil)

1 cup water

2-1/2 cups chicken broth

1 cup finely chopped onion

1 garlic clove, minced

4 Tbsp. olive oil

1 cup Arborio rice

1/4 cup freshly grated Parmesan

finely chopped fresh parsley for garnish

Simmer the tomatoes in the water for 1 minute. Drain them and reserve the liquid. Chop the tomatoes.

Combine the reserved tomato liquid and the broth. Bring to a simmer, and keep it at a bare simmer.

In a large saucepan cook the onion and the garlic in the oil over low heat, stirring constantly until they are softened.

Add the rice. Stir until each grain is coated with oil. Stir in the tomatoes.

Add 1/2 cup of the simmering liquid and cook the mixture over moderate heat, stirring constantly until the liquid is absorbed.

Continue adding the liquid, 1/2 cup at a time, stirring constantly and letting each portion be absorbed before adding the next.

The rice should take about 17 minutes to become al dente. Stir in the Parmesan and salt and pepper to taste.

Sprinkle the risotto with the parsley.

Makes 4 servings.

Robin Whitmore

RICE AND PEPPERS

Recipe from Noma Dizack

1 cup of Uncle Ben's Rice

1-2 cans of Ortega whole chile peppers, roasted and peeled

1 to 1-1/2 cups sour cream

salt, to taste

1-2 cups Jack cheese, grated

Cook rice according to package directions. Remove seeds and veins from peppers.

Mix cooked rice with sour cream.

Add salt to taste. Layer rice mixture in ovenproof bowl with jack cheese then peppers.

Repeat a second time.

Top with grated jack cheese.

Bake at 350° for 30 minutes.

Noma

SIMPLE RICE MOLD

rice

cheddar cheese

sour cream

Ortega peppers, diced

Mix cooked rice with grated cheddar cheese and sour cream.

Add diced Ortega peppers. Put into buttered mold.

Bake at 350° for 30 minutes.

PASTINA

Pastina
(if not available, substitute
with Israeli cous-cous)

1 onion, chopped

fresh thyme

2 cups of hot chicken broth

sun dried tomato tapenade

Parmesan cheese

Sauté onion in olive oil.

Stir in pastina and thyme.

Add 1-1/4 cup chicken broth and bring to boil. Cover.

Cook on low heat until broth is absorbed. Add more liquid until pasta is al dente.

When done, fluff and add sun dried tomato tapenade and cheese.

Brown Rice and Pine Nut Casserole

Recipe from Annie Denver

1/2 cup pine nuts

1/4 cup butter

1 cup brown rice, rinsed and drained

1/2 cup bulgur

1 large onion, chopped

1 cup minced fresh parsley

6 Tbsp. finely minced fresh chives or scallions

1/4 tsp. salt

1/4 tsp. pepper

3 (14-oz.) cans chicken broth

Sauté the pine nuts in a medium sized skillet with 2 tablespoons butter over moderate heat, until browned, about 5 minutes. Stir occasionally.

To the same skillet add and melt the remaining butter. Add the rice, bulgur and onion.

Brown for about 10 minutes, stirring frequently.

Spoon this mixture into a 2-quart casserole.

Add 3/4 cup parsley, chives, salt and pepper. Bring broth to a boil and stir into the rice mixture.

Bake uncovered in a preheated oven at 375° for 1-1/4 hours. Garnish with remaining parsley.

Annie is as beautiful as the song that bears her name.

FARFEL

1 8-oz. box Farfel
butter
1 onion, diced

Sauté one diced onion in butter for about 8 to 10 minutes.

Pour in one 8-oz. box Farfel. Mix well.

Cover with boiling water. Stir well.

Put uncovered into 350° oven.

After water is mostly absorbed, about 10 minutes, stir well and put back in oven for another 30 minutes. (If it looks dry, add more water before putting it back.)

Check every so often. If it sticks or looks dry, add a little water. Stir often.

Warm in oven, covered. When warm, remove cover.

Tess Braun

KOPITKA

Recipe from Judy's Polish housekeeper

Dumplings similar to gnocchi.

2 cups mashed potato
1 cup flour
1 egg
1/2 to 3/4 tsp. salt

Combine all the ingredients.

Knead on floured board.

Roll into long strips 3/4" in diameter.

Cut diagonally into 1" pieces. Boil in salted water 7-8 minutes.

Drain and serve with butter and salt, or drizzle with olive oil and sprinkle with grated parmesan.

Use same dough to make 1" balls. Deep fry in oil until golden brown.

Dough can also be cut into circles and wrapped around fruit. Boil 8 to 10 minutes.

Serve with sour cream and sugar.

Judy

My sister Patty, a wonderful hostess, has a marvelous cook. He is off on Sundays, so that's the day Patty prepares dinner for her children by herself. Below is her favorite Sunday night meal.

Mulberry Street Pizza
347 N. Canon Dr.
(310) 247-8998

They Deliver!

Patty

Patty: "Stick 'em up!"

Katie and Blake

ACCOMPANIMENTS

Arlene Grubman's Famous Jell-O Mold

Even people who say they don't like Jell-O like this. My sister Patty loves it!

2 (3-oz.) packages strawberry flavored Jell-O

1 cup water, boiling

2 (10-oz.) packages frozen sweetened strawberries, thawed

1 large 16-oz. can crushed pineapple, drained

4 medium sized bananas, mashed

2 cups coarsely chopped walnuts

2 cups sour cream

Combine Jell-O and boiling water and stir well to dissolve the Jell-O.

Blend in the thawed strawberries and juice, pineapple (well drained), mashed bananas, and nuts.

Pour half of the mixture into a 9" x 12" Pyrex dish. Cover and chill for 1-1/2 hours. Cover the remaining Jell-O mixture and let stand at room temperature.

When the refrigerated portion is firm, gently spread evenly with the sour cream.

Spoon the remaining Jell-O mixture evenly over the sour cream layer.

Cover and chill until firm, at least 4 hours.

Cut into squares and place on lettuce-lined plates.

My sister Patty at Eunice Knight Saunders School.

RIBBON JELL-O SQUARES

Recipe from Kim Pollard Grubman

1 pkg. large or 2 small lime Jell-O

1 pkg. large or 2 small strawberry or raspberry Jell-O

1/2 pint all purpose cream, whipping or half-and-half

1/2 pint sour cream

1/2 cup sugar

1 envelope unflavored gelatin

1/2 cup cold water

mayonnaise

Dissolve lime Jell-O in 3-1/2 cups boiling water. Set aside. Dissolve strawberry or raspberry Jell-O in 3-1/2 cups boiling water. Set aside. Do not refrigerate!

Note: you can use any 2 colors you choose. Mix unflavored gelatin in 1/2 cup cold water. Let stand 10 to 15 minutes to dissolve. Stir occasionally.

Pour all purpose cream into pot over very low flame. Add sugar slowly and stir. Add plain gelatin mixture to sugar and cream mixture.

Remove from stove and keep warm. (I put it in a double boiler with hot water. Otherwise it will firm up, which you don't want.)

Cream the sour cream for 2 minutes on low speed of mixer. Fold in sweet cream mixture. Slowly add sweet cream to sour cream while stirring.

Grease glass cake dish (14″ x 7″ x 2″) with mayonnaise. The glass pan allows you to see and follow the color layers; you will have about 17-18 layers altogether when finished!!!

Then put 1/2 to 2/3 cups of red Jell-O in glass dish. Refrigerate at least 30 minutes so bottom layer is extra firm.

Then take 1/2 to 2/3 cup of white gelatin mixture and place on top of red.

Refrigerate at least 20 minutes.

Then take 1/2 to 2/3 cup of green Jell-O mixture and layer on top of white. Refrigerate at least 20 minutes.

Continue as above, alternating red, white and green until all is used or until you're tired! When finished with the last layer, allow Jell-O to firm in refrigerator at least one hour.

This is a time consuming recipe, but it's great.

Hints:
Refrigerate glass dish before making Jell-O. I make 2 batches of the white gelatin (never seems to be enough).

You have to make 2 separate batches. Keep the white gelatin over warm water-it hardens faster than colored Jell-O.

Seymour and Kim

Apple Sauce

Apples
sugar, to taste
cinnamon, to taste

Cut apples in quarters. Peel.

Cut in half again.

Put apples in pan. Cover 1/2 full with water.

Add sugar.

Simmer until soft. Add cinnamon to taste.

Only 5 years old and I already knew how to give a "thumbs up."

Mom's Stewed Rhubarb

Recipe from Arlene Grubman

8-10 stalks of rhubarb, trimmed, cut into 1" pieces

2/3 cup sugar, plus more to taste

1/2 cup water

Place the rhubarb, sugar and water in a medium saucepan set over medium-low heat.

Simmer gently, stirring occasionally, until sugar is dissolved and rhubarb is almost tender, about 8 minutes. Cool immediately.

It is important that the rhubarb is cooked at a gentle simmer or it will quickly turn to mush.

Mom in Aspen. That's not a cigarette, it's a lollipop!

BRANDIED FRUIT

Recipe from Elly Kamm

Large can peach halves
with syrup

Large can pear halves
with syrup

Medium can dark cherries,
no syrup, drain well

1 lemon, sliced thin

Brandy, to taste

1 Tbsp. of butter

2 Tbsp. brown sugar

cornstarch*

Put all in saucepan. Heat. Add brandy to taste.

Can be assembled the night before and heated the following day.

If desired, use cornstarch to thicken.

Elly

CRANBERRY ORANGE SAUCE

Recipe from Arlene Grubman

Everyone loves this!

1 cup water

1/2 cup sugar

2 cups fresh cranberries

1/4 cup orange juice

2 tsp. cornstarch

2 tsp. grated orange rind

1/2 cup orange sections (or 1 can mandarin oranges)

For 4 servings: Combine water and sugar and bring to a boil. Boil for 5 minutes. Add cranberries and cook until they pop, about 5 minutes.

Combine orange juice and cornstarch. Stir until smooth. Add to cranberries.

Cook until clear and thickened. Stir in orange rind and sections. Serve with duck, chicken, meat, etc.

Mom – 1946

SMOKED TOMATO ANCHO CHILE MAYONNAISE

tomatoes, to be smoked and dried

mayonnaise

garlic roasted in olive oil

red onion, smoked for 1/2 hour

fresh lime juice

cayenne pepper

paprika

Ancho chile powder

olive oil

Dip tomato halves in red wine vinegar, then place in a smoker along with the red onion.

Smoke tomatoes until they are the consistency of dried fruit.

Smoke the red onion for 30 to 45 minutes.

Pour olive oil over garlic and roast or grill slowly for 1 hour.

Puree everything except mayonnaise in a food processor.

Mix equal amounts of tomato puree and mayonnaise.

Add lime juice and seasonings.

The exact quantities of ingredients for this recipe should be adjusted to your own taste.

Russian Mustard

1 cup dry mustard
(I use Colman's)

1 cup tarragon vinegar

2 eggs, slightly beaten

1 cup sugar

pinch of salt

Combine mustard and vinegar well and let sit covered, unrefrigerated for 12 hours.

Mix the eggs, sugar and salt with mustard mix and cook in a double boiler until it coats a spoon.

Cooks at least one hour.

Steven and Carrie

Parmesan Dip or Salad Dressing

1 cup sour cream

1/2 cup mayonnaise

1 cup (2 oz.) finely grated
Parmigiano or Reggiano

2-3 Tbsp. fresh lemon juice

1/2 tsp. black pepper

1/2 tsp. salt

Whisk all ingredients together in a bowl.

BBQ Sauce

1 (16-oz.) bottle of catsup

3/4 box brown sugar

1 large onion, diced

juice of one lemon

1 tsp. liquid smoke

1 Tbsp. teriyaki sauce

3 Tbsp. butter

2 Tbsp. vinegar

Cook onions in butter until tender.

Add other ingredients.

HOLLANDAISE SAUCE

Recipe from Mom

1 egg
2 egg yolks
3 Tbsp. water
3 Tbsp. lemon
1-1/2 cups melted butter

Beat egg and egg yolks with wire whisk.

Drizzle in water and lemon juice.

Beat with whisk over low-medium heat until hot.

Drizzle in melted butter, whisking constantly.

* Warning: Always be aware that raw and undercooked eggs can carry salmonella.

Steven and Carrie

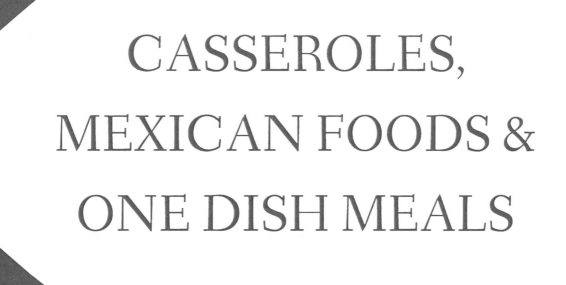

CASSEROLES, MEXICAN FOODS & ONE DISH MEALS

SHEPHERD'S PIE

Recipe from Annie Denver

2 lbs. ground beef or turkey

1 onion, diced

2 cans tomato soup

1-2 cups grated cheddar or Colby cheese

4-6 potatoes, unpeeled

Cook potatoes. Leave the skin on and mash with butter and salt.

Brown ground beef or turkey with onions. Line bottom of dish with it.

Cover with tomato soup.

Top with grated cheddar or Colby cheese.

Top with mashed potatoes.

Bake at 350° for 30 minutes.

* Yummy comfort food!

Annie and I have had some great adventures together.

MOUSSAKA
GREEK EGGPLANT-MEAT CASSEROLE

3 or 4 eggplants, peeled and cut into 1/4 inch thick slices

salted water

flour

1/2 cup (approx.) canola oil

2 Tbsp. olive oil

1 large onion, diced (1 cup)

2 tomatoes, peeled and diced or 2 cups canned plum tomatoes, drained

1-1/2 lbs. lean ground beef (substitute ground turkey if you like)

3/4 tsp. cinnamon

1/4 cup pine nuts, optional

1 tsp. salt

freshly ground pepper

1 cup or more freshly grated Parmesan cheese

Soak eggplant slices in salted water 20 minutes. Drain. Blot on paper towels. Coat with flour.

Preheat oven to 450°.

Cover rimmed baking sheet with heavy-duty foil. Coat foil with about 1/2 cup canola oil.

Add eggplant, turning to coat well. Bake about 20 minutes. Turn off oven and let eggplant stand another 30 minutes.

Heat olive oil in large skillet.

Add onion and sauté 1 minute. Add tomatoes and cook another minute.

Add beef and cinnamon and cook through.

Me with my two beautiful children, 1984

Custard Topping:

4 Tbsp. butter

5 Tbsp. flour

1/2 cup whipping cream

1 cup water

1/2 tsp. salt

freshly ground pepper

dash of nutmeg

2 eggs

2 tsp. fresh lemon juice

Steven performing at the Knitting Factory in Hollywood.

Add pine nuts if you are using them. Season to taste with salt and pepper.

Drain the meat, pour the drippings over the eggplant. Let meat cool while making the custard.

Casserole can be refrigerated or frozen before custard is added. Bring to room temperature before baking. Makes 6 to 8 servings

Custard Topping:

To make the custard, melt butter in medium skillet. Stir in flour and cook 1 minute.

Add cream, water, salt, pepper and nutmeg and cook until very thick, about 10 to 12 minutes, stirring frequently.

Remove from heat, cover and set aside.

Preheat oven to 350°. Grease 8"x15" casserole.

Layer eggplant and meat mixture to within 1" of top of casserole dish. Sprinkle each layer with some of the Parmesan cheese.

Bake 15 minutes. You may refrigerate or freeze before baking. Bring to room temperature before baking.

Beat eggs and whisk into cooled cream sauce. Add lemon juice. Taste and adjust seasoning. Spoon over casserole.

Continue baking on lowest shelf of oven until hot, browned and puffed, about 35 minutes. Cut into squares.

I have made this many times but I have always omitted the custard topping. This dish is delicious!

JOE'S SPECIAL

My version of this classic dish.

1 Tbsp. butter

1 Tbsp. olive oil

1 medium chopped onion

1 cup fresh mushrooms

1 lb. ground turkey breast

3 eggs, slightly beaten

1/2 tsp. granulated garlic

1 tsp. oregano

1 tsp. salt

1 tsp. freshly ground pepper

6 cups coarsely chopped fresh spinach or 2 pkgs. thoroughly drained frozen spinach

Melt butter and oil in large skillet.

Add onion and sauté briefly.

Mix in mushrooms and meat and cook until meat is brown.

Add eggs and seasonings and stir over medium heat until eggs are almost cooked.

Stir in spinach and cook a few minutes longer, until spinach is wilted.

Makes 3 servings.

Backstage at The Pageant of the Masters with Natali Galt.

TAMALE PIE

1 onion, chopped

1 large 7-oz. can diced green chilies

2 Tbsp. canola oil

1-1/2 lbs. ground lean beef or turkey

1 Tbsp. chili powder

1 cup bottled mild green or red taco sauce

3 cups cheddar shredded cheese

1 ripe avocado

1 tomato, chopped

sour cream

fresh chopped cilantro

Cornmeal Crust:

1-1/2 cups yellow cornmeal

3-1/2 cups water

1/2 teaspoon each ground cumin and salt

1/2 teaspoon cayenne pepper

In a 10" to 12" frying pan over medium heat, cook onion and chilies in oil, stirring occasionally until onion is limp, about 15 minutes. Set mixture aside.

In the same pan over high heat, brown meat with chili powder, breaking up with a spoon until meat is browned, about 10 minutes.

Skim off and discard the fat. Stir in onion mixture, half the taco sauce, and half the cheese. Spoon into crust. Can be made ahead to this point. Cover and chill overnight.

Bake uncovered in a 350° oven until hot in center, about 30 minutes, longer if chilled. Top with remaining cheese and bake until cheese melts, about 5 minutes longer. Garnish with avocado, tomato, sour cream and fresh cilantro. Put extra toppings in small bowls to pass around, along with taco sauce. Serves 6.

Cornmeal Crust:

In a 3 to 4 quart pot, combine cornmeal, water, ground cumin, salt, and cayenne pepper. Bring to a boil, stirring, and cook until mixture is thick enough to leave a path for 2 seconds when spoon is drawn through it (8 to 9 minutes).

Spread mixture evenly over bottom and 1" up sides of a shallow, ungreased 3-quart casserole.

Paella

1/4 cup olive oil

4 lbs. chicken, breasts, thighs and legs

1/3 cup flour

1 tsp. salt

1/8 tsp. freshly ground pepper

1/4 cup water

1 tsp. oregano

2 cups onion, chopped

3 cloves garlic, minced

3 Tbsp. butter

2 cups uncooked long grain white rice

4 tsp. powdered saffron

4 cups chicken stock

1/2 lb. Italian sausage, sliced

1 pkg. frozen artichoke hearts, thawed

2 cups peas

1 (28-oz.) can tomatoes, drained and coarsely chopped

1 lb. raw shrimp, shelled, deveined

24 cherrystone clams

Preheat oven to 350°. Heat olive oil in a large skillet. Dust chicken pieces with flour, salt and pepper. Brown well in oil.

Add 1/4 cup water and oregano.

Cover and cook chicken for 30 minutes over low heat. Remove chicken and set aside.

Add chopped onion and garlic to skillet and sauté, stirring, for 5 minutes. Set aside in skillet.

In a saucepan melt butter. Add rice and saffron. Stir over low heat for 5 minutes.

Add chicken stock, cover, and cook for 15 to 20 minutes.

Stir rice into skillet with onions. In a separate skillet, brown sausage lightly. Set aside.

In a 4 quart shallow casserole or paella pan, mix the artichoke hearts and peas with the rice, then lightly toss in the tomatoes, sausage, and shrimp. Arrange the chicken pieces on top.

Bake, uncovered for 30 minutes. Meanwhile, steam the clams in a separate pot, discarding any that do not open.

Place on top of casserole for the last 3 to 5 minutes of baking.

Taquitos

cooked brisket
1/2 onion chopped
12 corn tortillas
canola oil
sour cream

Avocado sauce:
1 avocado
3 Tbsp. water
2 Tbsp. lemon juice
1/8 tsp. salt
Green chile salsa

Combine shredded brisket and onion in skillet and cook, stirring to break up meat until most moisture is gone.

Let stand until cool enough to handle. Soften tortillas one at a time by placing in hot oil for a few seconds.

Place about 2 tablespoons meat on each tortilla and roll like a cigar, as tightly as possible.

Stack seam side down to keep from unrolling until ready to fry. You can refrigerate at this point. Cover them.

Heat 3/4-inch oil in 10" skillet.

Fry taquitos, seam side down, until crisp. Shake excess oil from taquitos, and place on paper-lined plate.

Place in oven at low temperature until all taquitos are cooked.

Serve with avocado sauce and sour cream.

Avocado sauce:
Whip avocado with water, lemon juice and salt until smooth. Add green chile salsa to taste.

Judy's Quesadillas

flour tortillas

Jack cheese

red grapes, sliced

cilantro

Fill flour tortillas with Jack cheese, sliced red grapes and cilantro. Sauté both sides in skillet until browned and cheese melts.

Easy Refried Beans

1/2 onion, chopped

1 small can Ortega chilies, diced

1 medium can of Rosarita refried beans

1 cup of grated Jack cheese

1 cup of grated cheddar cheese

Sauté onion in butter until onion is clear.

Add Ortega chilies and sauté 1 minute.

Add refried beans and heat thoroughly. Stir in 1/2 cup each of grated Jack cheese and cheddar cheese.

Pour into casserole.

Top with remaining grated Jack cheese and cheddar cheese. Put under broiler to melt cheese.

Wes

Susan and Wen

Judy and Andrea

Maria and Ken

Jose, Judy and Evan

Mark, Judy, Wes, Nathan & Marilyn, and Paul in Lucca, Italy.

BREAKFAST, BRUNCH, & SANDWICHES

SCRAMBLED EGGS WITH CAVIAR

6 uncooked large eggs in shells

5 Tbsp. whipping cream

2 Tbsp. chopped fresh chives

1/2 tsp. salt

1/2 tsp. freshly ground black pepper

3 Tbsp. butter

sour cream

caviar

whole fresh chives

Using egg topper or tip of small knife, cut a quarter-size hole in the wide end of each egg.

Empty 5 eggs into medium bowl.

Discard inside of remaining egg, or reserve for another use.

Rinse out 6 eggshells, and carefully wipe insides dry. Stand 6 shells, cut side up, in egg holders.

Whisk cream, chopped chives, salt and pepper into eggs.

Melt butter in heavy medium skillet over medium low heat.

Add egg mixture. Stir gently until mixture begins to set but is still soft, about 2 minutes.

Spoon egg mixture into shells.

Top with a little sour cream, then caviar.

Garnish with 2 pieces of 2" long whole chives.

Serve immediately.

Mom and me, ready for the opening night of *Wonderful Town*.

CHEESE STRATA

Great for brunch.

8 eggs

4 cups milk

1 tsp. salt

1/8 tsp. pepper

1/2 tsp. dry mustard

2 Tbsp. dry onion flakes

16 slices egg bread

12 oz. cheddar cheese, sliced

12 oz. Swiss cheese, sliced

Butter a 9" x 13" baking dish.

Trim crust from bread and place 8 slices on bottom of dish.

Cover with 6 oz. of cheddar and 6 oz. of Swiss cheese.

Sprinkle 1 Tbsp. onion over all.

Repeat with second layer of bread, cheese, and onion.

Beat eggs, milk, salt, pepper and mustard.

Pour over cheese mixture. Refrigerate overnight or at least 12 hours.

Bake at 350° for 1 hour or until puffed and lightly browned. Makes 10 servings.

Variation:
Add 1 can of Ortega Green Chilies to eggs.

Muesli

Not only is this delicious...it's healthy.

1 pound rolled oats

8 ounces chopped almonds

6 ounces chopped dried Mission figs

2 tsp. cinnamon

Mix all dry ingredients by hand. Store in container.

To Serve:
Soak 1 cup of mixture with almost the same amount of water overnight.

Next day add 1/2 crisp apple grated with skin.

Serve with low fat vanilla yogurt or plain yogurt.

(Left) The grand piano being delivered to my house on Smith Terrace in London. (Right) The second floor at 2 Smith Terrace.

SANTA FE RAILROAD FRENCH TOAST

When I was fifteen, my mom and I traveled to New York by train. We were so excited when the conductor said we were going to make a stop in Albuquerque, we went to our stateroom to prepare for the big adventure. We got so involved doing our hair and our make-up, we missed the stop. We may not have a memory of Albuquerque, but I will never forget this French toast. It's amazing!

5 slices day old white bread, cut 3/4" thick

6 eggs, lightly beaten

3 cups whipping cream

1/2 tsp. vanilla

1/4 tsp. salt

canola oil

powdered sugar

Cut bread slices diagonally in half. Beat the eggs with cream, vanilla and salt.

Dip bread into mixture and let soak at least 1 hour.

Heat canola oil until very hot (about 450°) in pan to a depth of 1".

Add 3 or 4 pieces of bread, or enough to fit the pan without crowding.

Fry until edges turn golden brown.

Turn and cook the other side just until the edges brown.

Remove and place on oven rack over a pan.

Bake at 400° for 3 to 5 minutes until puffy and golden.

Dust with powdered sugar.

Welsh Rabbit

Despite its name, this dish has nothing to do with rabbits. I learned to make it while I was working on "Wonderful Town" in London.

1 Tbsp. butter

1 Tbsp. flour

1/2 cup beer, preferable dark ale

1 Tbsp. Worcestershire sauce

1/2 dry English mustard

1/8 tsp. black pepper

3-1/2 cups cheddar cheese

1 egg

bread

Preheat broiler.

Over low heat, melt butter in a medium saucepan.

Whisk in flour and cook, stirring constantly for 1 minute.

Add beer, Worcestershire sauce, mustard, pepper and cheese.

Stir over medium heat until smooth and heated through.

Remove cheese mixture from heat and stir in a beaten egg yolk (optional).

Toast 8 pieces of bread on one side only, then arrange, toasted side down, in an ovenproof dish.

Pour cheese mixture over bread and brown under broiler for about 30 seconds.

Serve immediately. Makes 4 servings.

* If cheese is too thick, you can add a little milk or additional beer to thin it out.

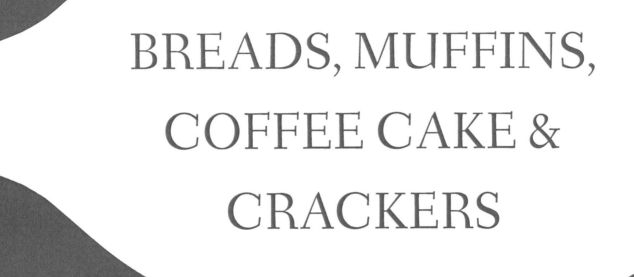

BREADS, MUFFINS, COFFEE CAKE & CRACKERS

GRANDMA MIRIAM'S MOHN KICHEL
(ONION AND POPPY SEED FLAT BREAD)

3-1/2 cups flour

2 tsp. baking powder

2 tsp. salt (can use a little less if you want, but use at least 1-3/4 tsp.)

1/4 cup poppy seeds

3/4 cup corn oil

2/3 cup cold water

1 onion, chopped fine

Mix the flour, baking powder, salt, and poppy seeds together. Then add corn oil, cold water, and chopped onion.

Mix well. Knead on well-floured board. The dough will absorb extra flour, but that's okay.

Keep flouring the board so dough doesn't stick. Roll it very thin. Separate into two portions.

Lay each half on an 11" x 15" non-stick cookie pan. Prick with fork and cut into squares.

Bake at 350° approximately 45 minutes, until it starts to turn brown.

Cool in pan.

Try this short cut. Eliminate the rolling pin, and press the dough firmly into the cookie pan. Stretch the dough until it is very thin. If there are holes in the dough from stretching too much, just keep pressing and rearranging the dough until it fits in the pan. Press it into the corners of the pan, too. It will be very thin, but that's okay.

GRANDMA MIRIAM'S CHALLAH

So good... and easy to make.

2 cakes yeast or
2 Tbsp. dry yeast

1-3/4 cup warm water

1 Tbsp. salt

1/2 cup sugar

1 cube melted butter (1/2 cup)

7 cups flour (3 cups, plus 4
cups)

4 large eggs, beaten

sesame seeds, or poppy seeds

1/4 cup melted butter, to brush
on bread dough before baking

In a large mixing bowl, dissolve yeast in water.

Add 1 Tbsp. of sugar. When it bubbles (about 5 minutes or longer) add salt, sugar and cube of melted butter.

Blend in 3 cups of flour.

Then add the eggs and beat thoroughly. Add 4 cups of flour and mix.

If you have a Kitchen Aid mixer, put dough hook on and mix 4 minutes to knead. Otherwise, turn out on a floured board and knead until smooth and elastic.

Pour a bit of the melted butter in a large bowl and wipe the interior of the bowl with it.

Place dough into the buttered bowl, cover, let rise until doubled.

Punch down and turn it out again onto a floured board. Divide in half.

Cut one half into 3 equal pieces and roll into strips about 18" long.

Braid these strips and place this large braid on a buttered cookie sheet.

Divide the remaining dough into 2 parts, 2/3 and 1/3.

Divide the 2/3 part into 3 equal pieces and roll out into strips.

Braid. Place braid on top of first braid that is on cookie sheet.

Form the remaining 1/3 dough into another braid. Or just twist the strip. Lay it over the first 2 braids.

Once braids are stacked, brush with melted butter.

Don't brush butter onto braids before you stack them, or the upper braids will slide off.

Cover and let rise again until doubled.

Brush again with melted butter. Sprinkle heavily with seeds.

Bake at 350° for 45 minutes to 1 hour.

You can also make 2 smaller loaves with 2 layers, or 3 loaves with 1 level.

Morris and Miriam Grubman

Pita Parmesan

pita bread
melted butter
freshly grated Parmesan cheese

Preheat oven to 400°.

Using sharp knife, split pita in half horizontally as you would an English muffin.

Brush rough sides generously with melted butter and sprinkle with Parmesan.

Cut into quarters, transfer to a baking sheet and broil until golden.

Judy's Blue Ribbon Banana Bread

1 cup all-purpose flour plus 3/4 cup almond flour*
1-1/2 tsp. baking soda
3/4 tsp. kosher salt
3 large eggs
1-1/2 cups sugar
2 large ripe bananas, mashed (if bananas are small, use 3)
1/2 cup canola oil
1 cup chopped walnuts (optional)

Preheat oven to 350°. Grease two 9" x 5" x 3" loaf pans with nonstick spray or canola oil. Thoroughly combine flour, baking soda, and salt in a medium bowl. Whisk eggs, sugar, bananas, and oil in a large bowl until smooth. Add dry ingredients to banana mixture. Stir just until combined. Stir in walnuts. Pour batter into prepared pans.

Bake until brown, approximately 40 to 45 minutes. Cool. Run knife around inside edge of pan, then invert onto a serving plate. Turn bread right side up and serve.

*If you don't have almond flour, use 1-3/4 cups all-purpose flour.

Blueberry Muffins
with Lemon Crunch Topping

1-3/4 cups flour

1/3 cup wheat germ

1/3 cup sugar

3 tsp. baking powder

1/2 tsp. salt

1 cup milk

1/4 cup canola oil

1 egg

1 cup fresh blueberries, washed and dried (can substitute well drained frozen berries)

3 Tbsp. sugar

3 tsp. grated lemon peel

Combine flour, wheat germ, 1/3 cup sugar, baking powder and salt in a bowl. Mix well.

Combine milk, oil and egg and beat lightly.

Add to dry ingredients all at once and stir just until dry ingredients are moistened.

Fold in blueberries.

Fill paper-lined or greased muffin pans 2/3 full of batter.

Combine remaining 3 tablespoons sugar and lemon peel. Sprinkle on top of batter.

Bake at 425° for 20 to 25 minutes. Makes 1 dozen medium muffins.

Pumpkin Nut Cake

3 eggs

1 pound can of pumpkin

3/4 cup canola oil

1/2 cup water

2-1/2 cups all purpose flour

2-1/4 cup sugar

1-1/2 tsp. baking soda

1-1/4 tsp. salt

3/4 tsp. nutmeg

3/4 tsp. cinnamon

1 cup yellow raisins

1/2 cup chopped walnuts

For the icing:

4 oz. cream cheese

3 Tbsp. butter

1 tsp. lemon juice or vanilla

1/2 of a 16 oz. box confectioners sugar

Beat the eggs, pumpkin, canola oil, and water together.

Then add into the mixture the flour, sugar, baking soda, salt, nutmeg, cinnamon, yellow raisins, and walnuts.

Pour into buttered pan. Bake at 350° for 2 hours. Cool cakes and frost with icing:

For the icing, beat all ingredients. Frost cake. Sprinkle with chopped walnuts.

Judy's Sour Cream Coffee Cake

2 sticks butter (1 cup)

2 cups sugar

2 eggs

2 cups flour, sifted

1/2 tsp. vanilla

1 tsp. baking powder

1 cup sour cream (8 oz.)

Topping:

1/2 cup chopped walnuts

1/2 tsp. cinnamon

2 tsp. brown sugar

Cream together butter and sugar.

Add eggs one at a time. Stir in sour cream and vanilla.

In a separate bowl, sift flour with baking powder. Stir into butter/sugar mixture.

Pour 1/2 of the batter into well-greased and floured tube pan.

Sprinkle 1/2 of the topping over cake. Add remaining batter and sprinkle with the rest of the topping.

Bake for 350° for 1 hour and 15 minutes.

Nanny Arlene's Monkey Bread

In the 1960's and 1970's, my mother served this at all her dinner parties.

2 cups milk
1/3 cup sugar
1/2 cup shortening
1/4 cup warm water
1 pkg. dry yeast
5 cups sifted flour
1 tsp. baking soda
1 tsp. baking powder
2-1/2 tsp. salt
1/2 cup butter, melted

Heat milk, and mix in sugar and shortening.

Cool to lukewarm temperature. Dissolve yeast in warm water. Let rest for 5 minutes.

Add to milk mixture. Beat in 3 cups flour by hand.

Cover with cloth and let rise for 2 hours in a warm place.

Sift remaining flour with baking soda, powder and salt, and work into dough.

Cover and let rise for another hour in a warm place.

Turn the dough out onto a well-floured surface and spread out with hands.

Pinch off pieces of dough, and make 1-1/2" to 2" diameter balls. Dip each ball in melted butter and arrange side by side in a bundt or tube pan making several layers.

Cover pan and let rise again until double in size, about 45 minutes to an hour.

Bake 350° for 45 to 55 minutes.

Zucchini Bread

Recipe from Andrea Bernard

2 cups sugar

1 cup canola oil

3 large eggs

1 Tbsp. cinnamon

1 tsp. baking powder

1 tsp. baking soda

1 tsp. vanilla

1/2 tsp. ground ginger

1/2 tsp. salt

3-1/4 cup sifted all purpose flour

3 cups shredded, unpeeled zucchini, approx. 3 medium

1 cup walnuts, ground

Preheat oven to 325°. Grease two 8" x 4" inch loaf pans generously with shortening. Line the pans with wax paper and grease it.

Stir baking powder and baking soda into flour. Combine all the ingredients except the flour mixture, zucchini and walnuts. Beat for 2 minutes until blended, scraping side of bowl. Fold in flour until blended, then fold in the zucchini and walnuts.

Pour into pans. Bake on a center rack approximately 50 minutes.

Andrea and Judy in Lucca, Italy, 2007.

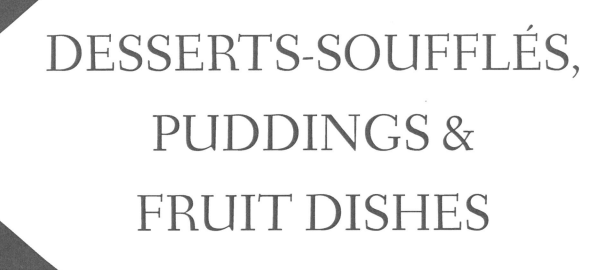

DESSERTS-SOUFFLÉS, PUDDINGS & FRUIT DISHES

CHOCOLATE NUT SOUFFLÉ

Recipe from Arlene Grubman

4 (1 oz.) squares of semi-sweet chocolate

8 Tbsp. sugar

1 envelope unflavored gelatin

1/4 tsp. salt

1 cup milk

5 eggs, separated

1/4 cup rum (Mom used Grand Marnier)

1 tsp. vanilla

1/4 cup coarsely chopped walnuts

1 cup whipping cream

Judy–

I did not use the second cup of whipped cream for garnish. Although I did double the recipe. This can be made the day before. The nuts make it different from any other souffle.

Absolutely fantastic.

Love, Mom

Melt chocolate over very low heat in a double boiler. Remove from heat.

Stir in 6 Tbsp. sugar, gelatin and salt. Gradually add milk, stirring to keep mixture smooth.

Beat egg yolks slightly, then add a little chocolate mixture to the egg yolks, then add yolk mixture to chocolate mixture.

Cook over low heat, stirring constantly until mixture begins to boil.

Remove from heat. Stir in rum or Grand Marnier.

Stir in vanilla and coarsely chopped nuts. Chill until slightly thickened, stir occasionally.

Beat egg whites until stiff, but not dry.

Whip one cup of whipping cream and carefully fold into chocolate mixture with egg whites.

Pour into 3 cup soufflé dish. Chill until firm.

Before serving whip 1 cup whipping cream with remaining 2 Tbsp. sugar.

Garnish soufflé with whipped cream and sprinkle with finely chopped nuts. Makes 6 to 8 servings.

STRAWBERRY DELIGHT

This recipe came from an employee of Braun Jewelers. It really is delightful.

2 small packages strawberry Jell-O

2-1/2 cups boiling water

1 angel food cake

2-3 boxes of fresh strawberries (can also use frozen strawberries)

whipping cream

Pour water over Jell-O, stir to dissolve and place in refrigerator until half-set.

Halve fresh strawberries and stir them into the Jell-O. You can use a combination of fresh and frozen strawberries.

Whip 1 pint of whipping cream and fold into the Jell-O. Cut Angel Food cake into small squares.

Line bottom of dish with cake, then pour Jell-O and whipped cream mixture over cake.

Repeat with second layer. Cover and refrigerate overnight.

BULL MOUSSE

A very rich chocolate mousse.

1 lb. good quality bittersweet chocolate

2 eggs

1 pint whipping cream

Melt the bittersweet chocolate over water in a double boiler.

Allow to cool somewhat (though still melted).

Beat in the eggs and whipping cream with a mixer at moderate speed until smooth.

Set in a freezer several hours until hard.

This is a very rich dessert. Portions should be small.

Patty

Chocolate Mousse

Recipe from Noma Dizack

5 squares of semi-sweet chocolate

3 Tbsp. water

4 egg yolks

1/2 cup plus 2 Tbsp. SUPER FINE sugar

1 Tbsp. brandy

5 egg whites

1/4 tsp. cream of tartar

10 chocolate shells or champagne glasses

Combine chocolate squares and water in top of double boiler. Melt, stirring occasionally. Set aside to cool.

Beat egg yolks, add super fine sugar and beat until pale yellow.

Add cooled melted chocolate to egg mixture, beat until well blended.

Stir in brandy.

Beat egg whites with cream of tartar until stiff peaks form.

Add 1 cup of egg white to the chocolate mixture, then fold in the rest of the egg whites.

Pour into chocolate shells or champagne glasses.

Chill several hours.

"Out of This World" Lemon Soufflé

Recipe from Arlene Grubman

2 envelopes Knox gelatin

1/2 cup water

6 pasteurized eggs

1-1/2 cups sugar

2 cups whipping cream

1 Tbsp. grated lemon rind

2/3 cup fresh lemon juice

Arlene

During World War II, Mom worked at the Hollywood Canteen.

Prepare a 4 cup soufflé dish with a foil collar.

Sprinkle gelatin over water in a small saucepan. Let stand 10 minutes, until gelatin is softened. Place pan over very low heat until gelatin dissolves. Mixture will be clear. Remove from heat and cool.

Combine eggs and sugar in large bowl of electric mixer or use a hand electric mixer. Beat mixture at high speed until very thick and light.

Whip 1-1/2 cups of the cream in a small bowl until soft peaks form. Refrigerate.

Combine lemon rind and lemon juice with cooled gelatin. Pour into the egg mixture. Continue beating until well blended. Remove bowl from mixer. Chill briefly (5 minutes) in refrigerator. Stir often, just until mixture is thick enough to mound.

Fold in whipped cream with a rubber scraper until no streaks of white remain. Pour into prepared dish. Refrigerate at least 3 hours or until set. Remove collar gently, if necessary use a small paring knife.

Beat remaining cream. Garnish soufflé with whipped cream and mint sprigs and lemon twists. Makes 8 servings.

* Can be prepared in individual ramekins.

Grape-Nut Pudding

Recipe from Janet DeCarolis

4-5 eggs, well beaten

2/3 cup sugar

1/2 tsp. salt

1 tsp. vanilla

3 cups hot milk

1/2 cup grape-nuts (use a little more, if desired)

1/2 cup raisins (optional)

1/2 tsp. nutmeg

Mix eggs, sugar, salt, vanilla, and nutmeg.

Add hot milk, grape-nuts, and raisins.

Pour into a 2 quart casserole.

Set in a pan of hot water about 1-1/2" deep.

Bake at 325° for 50 to 60 minutes.

Insert a knife and check before time is up to see if it's done. If the knife comes out clean it's done.

Top with whipped cream.

Janet likes it while it's still warm.

Janet

Frozen Grand Marnier Soufflé

3 pasteurized egg whites whipped with a pinch of salt until stiff

1 cup whipping cream, whipped

1 Tbsp. grated orange rind (approx. 2 oranges)

1/2 gallon French vanilla ice cream

1/4-1/2 cup Grand Marnier (or more, if desired)

Combine ice cream, orange rind, and Grand Marnier, then fold in egg whites and whipping cream.

Put in freezer for 10 minutes.

Then put in a soufflé dish with a collar.

Dust top with powdered cocoa.

Judy

Apple Cobbler

For filling:

1/2 cup sugar

1-1/2 Tbsp. flour

1/4 cup unsalted butter

3 lb. apples, peeled, cored and sliced

2 Tbsp. fresh lemon juice

1 tsp. vanilla

For crust:

2 cups all-purpose flour

1/4 cup sugar

2 tsp. baking powder

1/4 tsp. salt

2 Tbsp. unsalted butter, chilled and cut into small cubes

1/3 cup chopped crystallized ginger

1 Tbsp. grated orange rind

1 cup heavy cream, plus more for brushing

For filling:

Combine sugar and flour. Melt butter over medium heat. Stir in apples, lemon juice, sugar and flour mixture and cook 15 to 20 minutes.

Partially cover pan. When apples are tender, remove from heat and stir in vanilla. Cool, then transfer to buttered 1-1/2 quart baking dish.

For crust:

Mix flour, sugar, baking powder and salt in a bowl. With a pastry blender or your fingers, cut in butter until mixture resembles coarse crumbs.

Stir in ginger. Combine cream and orange zest. Stir cream-zest mixture into flour mixture, just until it holds together. Gather into a ball and knead on floured board until soft. Roll out a little larger than the baking dish.

Top apples with pastry and trim off excess. Cut a few small holes in pastry for steam to escape. Cut out leftover pastry into fancy designs and decorate the crust. Attach pastry designs with cream.

Bake at 425° for 10 minutes. Reduce heat to 375° and bake another 20 to 25 minutes or until golden.

Cool. Serve warm with ice cream or whip cream. Makes 6 to 8 servings.

APPLE CRISP

6 apples, peeled, and sliced or roughly chopped

1/2 cup water

1 to 1-1/2 tsp. cinnamon

1 cup flour

1 stick butter (1/2 cup)

1 cup granulated sugar

1/3 cup brown sugar

Place apples into greased baking dish.

Pour water over apples.

Sprinkle with cinnamon.

With a fork, work together flour, butter and sugars until crumbly.

Sprinkle mixture over apples.

Bake at 375° for 40 to 45 minutes.

Judy

Sugar Crusted Apples

6 large baking apples
2/3 cup granulated sugar
1/3 cup all purpose flour
1/2 tsp. cinnamon
1/3 cup butter
1 egg
3/4 cup apple cider

Preheat oven to 350°.

Core and peel apples. In a bowl mix flour, sugar and cinnamon with fork or pastry blender.

Cut in butter. Beat egg slightly. Brush egg on apples.

Coat apples with sugar mixture.

Place apples in greased shallow baking dish.

Fill centers with remaining sugar mixture.

Pour cider in bottom of dish.

Bake 1 hour, or until apples are tender.

Judy

MOTHER BAKER'S APPLE DUMPLINGS

This recipe is from Wes's grandmother, Aileen Baker. Wes's dad always called her "Mother Baker." She was born in 1889, and was one of the few women of her era to graduate from college.

For Syrup*:

1-1/2 cups sugar (2-1/4 cups)

1-1/2 cups of water (2-1/4 cups)

1/4 tsp. cinnamon (scant 1/2 tsp.)

1/4 tsp. nutmeg (1/2 tsp.)

3-4 drops red food color

3 Tbsp. butter (5 Tbsp.)

For Dumplings:

2 cups sifted flour

2 tsp. baking powder

1 tsp. salt

2/3 cup shortening

1/2 cup milk

6 medium whole apples, pared and cored

* For more syrup, use the quantities in parentheses.

Combine sugar, water, cinnamon, nutmeg, and food color. Bring to boil. Add butter.

Sift together flour, baking powder and salt. Cut in shortening.

Add milk all at once and stir just until flour is moistened.

On lightly floured surface, roll 1/8 inch thick into 18" x 12" rectangle. Cut with knife or pastry wheel into 6" squares.

Place 1 whole apple in each square. Sprinkle each apple generously with sugar, cinnamon, and nutmeg. Dot apples with butter.

Moisten edges of squares. Fold corners to center and pinch edges together. Place 1" apart in ungreased 8" x 11" baking dish or pan.

Pour syrup over dumplings and sprinkle with sugar.

Bake in moderate oven (375°) for 35 minutes or till apples are done. Serve warm. Pour syrup over dumplings and sprinkle with sugar. Serve with whipped cream or vanilla ice cream.

CHARLOTTE RUSSE

Recipe from Andrea Bernard

2 envelopes unflavored gelatin

3/4 cup sugar

1/4 tsp. salt

2 cups milk

4 slightly beaten egg yolks, at room temperature

1 cup sour cream

2 tsp. vanilla

12 ladyfingers, split

4 stiffly-beaten egg whites

1 cup whipping cream

raspberry sauce

fresh raspberries for garnish

Raspberry Sauce:

2 (10 oz.) pkg. of frozen raspberries

2 Tbsp. cornstarch

1 (8 oz.) jar currant jelly or raspberry jelly

In a 9" springform pan, arrange split ladyfingers, sliced even on one side, around edge of pan. You can also use a Charlotte Russe mold and arrange the ladyfingers on the bottom and sides in an interesting pattern.

In a medium saucepan combine gelatin, sugar, salt and milk and let gelatin soften.

When gelatin is softened, cook and stir over low heat.

Add a tablespoon of the heated liquid to the egg yolks then add yolks slowly to milk mixture in saucepan.

Stir constantly at low temperature until mixture coats a spoon.

Remove from heat and stir in sour cream and vanilla. Chill until mixture mounds slightly.

Fold beaten egg whites gently into chilled gelatin mixture and then fold whipped cream into the mixture.

Pour into mold and chill overnight or until firm.

To serve, unmold on platter and drizzle with raspberry sauce and garnish with fresh raspberries. Makes 12 servings.

With Andrea at Las Ventanas in Cabo San Lucas.

Raspberry Sauce:

Thaw and crush raspberries.

In saucepan, combine with cornstarch and jelly.

Cook and stir till bubbly. Strain and cool. Chill.

Makes about 2-1/4 cups.

You can also just strain the frozen raspberries and add sugar to taste as an alternative to the raspberry sauce.

Variations:

Fold 3/4 cup flaked or shredded coconut into gelatin mixture.

Fold 2 Tbsp. grated lemon rind into gelatin mixture.

DESSERTS-PIES, TARTS & CAKES

BLUEBERRY GALETTE

Recipe from Jennifer Hein

1 lb. fresh blueberries, 3 cups

2 Tbsp. cornstarch

1 Tbsp. finely grated fresh lemon zest, plus more for garnish

1 Tbsp. fresh lemon juice

1/4 tsp. ground cinnamon

1/4 tsp. salt

1/2 cup sugar, plus 1 tsp. sugar

1 package refrigerated pie dough (enough for a 9" pie)

1 Tbsp. cold unsalted butter, cut into pieces

1 large egg, lightly beaten

Put oven rack in middle position and preheat oven to 425°. Line a large baking sheet with foil and butter the foil. Stir together blueberries, cornstarch, lemon zest, lemon juice, cinnamon, salt and 1/2 cup of sugar in a large bowl until combined.

Unwrap pie dough and unfold onto baking sheet. Spoon blueberry mixture onto center of dough, leaving 1-1/2" border around the edge.

Fold edge of dough over 1" of blueberry mixture, pleating dough. Dot the blueberry filling with butter pieces.

Lightly brush pastry with some of the beaten egg and sprinkle with a teaspoon of sugar and a bit more lemon zest. Bake until blueberry filling is bubbling and pastry is golden, 25 to 30 minutes. Cool slightly on baking sheet on a rack.

Serve warm galette with ice cream or fresh whipped cream.

This recipe takes about 10 minutes to make, but looks like a very fancy dessert. It can be made the day of a party and served slightly warmed or at room temperature.

Happy Eating!

Jennifer and Judy

VANILLA CREAM PIE

WITH FLAVOR VARIATIONS

Recipe from Marilyn Kassler

3/4 cup sugar

3 heaping tsp. cornstarch

1/4 tsp. salt

2 cups milk

3 slightly beaten egg yolks

2 Tbsp. butter

1 tsp. vanilla

1 9" baked pastry pie shell

Preheat oven to 350°.

In saucepan, combine sugar, cornstarch and salt. Gradually stir in milk.

Cook and stir constantly over medium heat until mixture boils and thickens.

Cook 2 minutes longer. Remove from heat.

Stir small amount of hot mixture into egg yolks, then add egg yolks to hot mixture.

Cook 2 minutes, stirring constantly.

Remove from heat.

Add butter and vanilla.

Cool to room temperature.

To prevent a crust from forming, spread saran wrap on top of pudding.

Pour through sieve into baked pie shell.

Marilyn

Flavor Variations

Chocolate Cream Pie:

In Vanilla Cream Pie filling, increase sugar to 1 cup. Chop 2 (1 oz.) squares of unsweetened chocolate, add with milk.

Banana Cream Pie:

Slice 3 bananas into cooled 9" baked pastry shell. Top with Vanilla Cream Pie filling and meringue or whipped cream.

Coconut Cream Pie:

Add 1 cup flaked coconut to Vanilla Cream Pie filling. When cool, top with whipped cream. Sprinkle with 1/3 cup toasted coconut.

Pastry Pie Shell

1-1/2 cups pastry flour, measure and sift into bowl

1/2 tsp. salt

1/2 cup shortening

2 Tbsp. cold water

With a fork, mix flour and salt with shortening in medium bowl until crumbly.

Sprinkle with water until it forms a ball. Pour into ungreased pie tin.

Flatten to tin with flowered fingers. Prick with fork.

Bake at 450° for 10-12 minutes.

OPEN FACE PEACH PIE

Recipe from Frances Whitmore

This is out of this world!

3/4 cup sugar

2 Tbsp. flour

1/8 tsp. cinnamon

sour cream

6-8 large fresh peach halves
(preferably peaches with pink
centers)

1 unbaked piecrust

Mix sugar, flour, and cinnamon and add just enough sour cream to make a thin paste.

Place peach halves cut side up in unbaked pie shell.

Fill in the cracks with small peach pieces. Cover with sour cream mixture.

Bake 450° for 10 minutes; then 350° about 30 minutes or until cream mixture becomes slightly brown.

*This recipe dates back to Wes's grandmother Whitmore and is delicious.

Frances

FRANCES WHITMORE'S DELUXE PECAN PIE

1 unbaked pastry shell

3 eggs

1 cup dark Karo syrup

2/3 cup sugar

1/4 cup butter, melted

1 tsp. vanilla

1/8 tsp. salt

1 cup pecan halves

Beat eggs slightly.

Mix in next 5 ingredients, then add nuts. Pour into pie shell.

Bake at 350° for 55-65 minutes. Filling should be slightly less set in center than around edge.

Tip from Frances:
Toast pecans slightly, about 5 minutes in 350° oven before using. Watch them closely. This recipe may be my one claim to fame. Anyone can make the filling but it deserves a good crust!

Katie and Judy at Steven and Carol's wedding.

Applesauce Spice Cake

This is one of my all-time favorite recipes. When we lived in Aspen, I used to bake it for Steven's and Carrie's birthdays.

2-1/2 cups flour

2 cups sugar

1-1/2 tsp. baking soda

1-1/2 tsp. salt

1/4 tsp. baking powder

3/4 tsp. cinnamon

1/2 tsp. cloves

1/2 tsp. allspice

1-1/2 cups applesauce

1/2 cup water

1/2 cup shortening

2 eggs

3/4 cup chopped walnuts

Butter Frosting:

1/3 cup butter, softened

3 cups confectioners sugar

1-1/2 tsp. vanilla

2 Tbsp. milk (may need to use a little more if frosting is too thick)

few drops red food color

Preheat oven to 350°.

Grease and flour a 9″ x 13″ x 2″ pan. Measure all ingredients into large mixer bowl.

Blend 30 seconds on low speed, scraping bowl constantly.

Beat 3 minutes on high speed, scraping bowl occasionally.

Pour batter into pan. If there is any extra batter, pour into paper lined muffin cups.

Bake cupcakes 25 to 30 minutes. Bake layer cake 50 to 55 minutes. Cool. Frost with butter frosting.

Butter Frosting:
Blend butter and confectioners sugar. Beat in vanilla, milk and a few drops of food color. Blend until smooth.

Judy in Aspen

CHEESE CAKE

This is from an old friend who made me promise never to share the recipe. Uh-oh.

Crust:

1-1/2 cups graham cracker crumbs

3 Tbsp. sugar

1/3 cup butter

Filling:

1 (20 oz.) can crushed pineapple, well drained, nearly dry

3 (8 oz.) packages of cream cheese, softened

4 eggs (if small eggs, use 5)

1/2 cup sugar

Topping:

1/2 pint sour cream

1 tsp. vanilla

4 Tbsp. sugar

Crust:

Combine ingredients and press firmly into a springform pan.

Filling:

Beat sugar and cream cheese first. Then add 1 egg at a time. Spread pineapple over crust.

Pour cheese mixture over pineapple. Bake in 350° oven, 30 to 35 minutes.

Remove cheese cake from oven.

Topping:

Combine sour cream, vanilla and sugar, and gently spread mixture over cheese cake.

Return to oven for 5 minutes. Remove from oven.

Let chill 3 hours.

Judy in Venice

SUPER CARROT CAKE

* I like to bake some of this batter in mini muffin pans. Each muffin is about two bites.

2 cups flour (sift first, then measure)

2 tsp. baking soda

1/4 tsp. nutmeg

1/2 tsp. salt

2 tsp. cinnamon

1/2 tsp. cloves

3 eggs

3/4 cup oil

3/4 cup buttermilk

2 cups sugar

2 tsp. vanilla

8 oz. can crushed pineapple, drained (reserve juice)

2 cups grated carrots

3-1/2 oz. shredded coconut

1 cup chopped walnuts

Frosting (if desired):

2 oz. soft cream cheese

3-4 Tbsp. of reserved pineapple juice

4-5 cups sifted powdered sugar

1 tsp. vanilla

Sift together the flour, baking soda, nutmeg, salt, cinnamon, and cloves in a bowl. Set aside.

Beat together the above ingredients.

Begin by beating the eggs. Add the oil, beat well.

Add the buttermilk, beat well. Add the sugar and vanilla, beat well.

Blend the dry ingredients into this mixture.

Add the following to the batter: crushed pineapple, grated carrots, shredded coconut, and chopped walnuts.

Bake in a 9" x 13" pan, or bunt pan. Bake approximately 55 minutes at 350°.

Frosting (if desired):

Beat the cream cheese and pineapple juice. Add powdered sugar and vanilla. Beat until fluffy.

Chocolate Pudding Cake

I first had this at a sorority house at the University of Arizona. It's a combination of crunchy brownies and chocolate pudding. Serve warm with a spoon.

Non-stick vegetable spray

1 cup all-purpose flour

1/2 cup unsweetened Dutch-process cocoa, divided

2 tsp. baking powder

1/4 tsp. salt

3/4 cup granulated sugar

3/4 cup chopped walnuts or pecans

3/4 cup milk

2 tsp. vanilla extract, divided

2 Tbsp. unsalted butter, melted

1 cup lightly packaged light-brown sugar

1-3/4 cup hot water

Adjust oven rack to middle position and preheat to 350°. Lightly coat a 2-quart baking dish with vegetable spray.

In a large bowl, sift flour, 1/4 cup cocoa, baking powder, salt and granulated sugar.

Stir in nuts, milk, 1 tsp. vanilla and melted butter. Spread batter in prepared pan.

In small bowl, mix brown sugar and remaining 1/4 cup cocoa. Sprinkle over batter.

In another small bowl, mix hot water and remaining vanilla; pour over cocoa mixture.

Bake 30 minutes, or until top layer is set and cake just starts to pull from sides.

Keep warm.

Makes 8 servings.

Camping in the snow!

SUMMER BLUEBERRY CAKE

This was a favorite summer dessert when we lived in Aspen.

1/2 cup butter
1 cup sugar
1/4 tsp. salt
1 tsp. vanilla
2 eggs, separated
1-1/2 cups plus 1 Tbsp. flour
1 tsp. baking powder
1/3 cup milk
1 cups fresh blueberries

Cream butter and 3/4 cup sugar.

Add salt and vanilla. Add egg yolks, beat until creamy.

Sift 1-1/2 cups flour and baking powder; add alternately with milk to egg yolk mixture.

Beat egg whites until stiff, adding remaining 1/4 cup sugar.

Coat berries with 1 Tbsp. flour, add to batter. Fold in egg whites.

Pour into a greased 8" square pan. Sprinkle with granulated sugar.

Bake at 350° for 50 minutes.

Nan, Andrea, Judy, and Steven

Marcia's Grandma Rose's Apple Cake

Recipe from my cousin Marcia

This cake was always served on Shabbat and special occasions by her Grandma Rose.

4-6 apples, depending on size
1/2 cup butter-flavored Crisco
1 cup sugar
2 eggs
1 Tbsp. orange juice
1 tsp. vanilla
1 cup flour
1 tsp. baking powder
cinnamon
butter

Mix Crisco and sugar until fluffy.

Add eggs one at a time.

Add orange juice and vanilla to mixture.

Sift flour and baking powder and add to mixture.

Pour mixture into a 9" greased and floured cake pan.

Peel apples and cut into 1/8" slices.

Gently press apples into dough in a circular design, rounded side up.

Sprinkle with cinnamon and dot with butter.

Bake at 350° for 45 to 50 minutes.

Sprinkle with powdered sugar before serving.

Marcia

Gingerbread

Recipe from Carrie Braun Jabs

While my daughter Carrie attended Menlo College, she worked at a local restaurant. Aside from waitressing, one of her responsibilities was to bake this gingerbread. It's delicious!

1/2 cup butter
1/2 cup sugar
1 egg
1 cup molasses
2-1/2 cups flour
1-1/2 tsp. baking soda
1/2 tsp. salt
1 heaping tsp. ground ginger
1 tsp. cinnamon
1/2 tsp. ground cloves
1 cup hot water

Preheat oven to 350°.

Cream butter and sugar. Add egg and molasses. Blend well.

Blend dry ingredients together and add to egg/molasses mixture.

Add hot water and beat until smooth.

Pour into greased 9" cake pan.

Bake approx. 30 minutes, or until toothpick comes out clean.

Carrie, Graduation.

Carrie at ballet

Carrie and Mike
November 8, 1997

SPECIALTY PASTRIES

Mandeltarta, Swedish Almond Torte
with Orange Cream Filling

Recipe from my brother Billy who is a wonderful cook

2/3 cup ground blanched almonds (1 package slivered)

1/2 cup sugar

1/2 cup soft butter

1 Tbsp. flour

2 Tbsp. cream

1 (1 oz.) square semi-sweet baking chocolate, grated

orange cream filling

strawberries

Combine almonds, sugar, butter, flour and cream until well blended.

Cover 3 cookie sheets with aluminum foil. Leave ends loose, "floating" on top of cookie sheets.

Using an 8" plate as a guide, draw a circle around the plate onto the foil in the center of the cookie sheet. This will help you to shape the dough.

Divide almond dough into 3 equal portions. Spread each in a thin circle on one foil covered sheet.

Turn up the edges of the foil slightly, as the dough spreads widely during baking. Bake each sheet separately in the oven at 375°. Bake for 4 minutes until very soft.

With a long metal spatula, smooth the edges of the dough into the 8" circles you have drawn. Continue baking about 3 to 4 minutes longer.

Watch it during baking. It will bubble and bubble all over. When it stops bubbling (or nearly so) it will be quite brown and done.

Watch it carefully and do not over bake as the dark brown edges will be bitter.

Remove aluminum foil from cookie sheets by sliding it off onto a flat counter or table. Allow it to cool 1 to 2 hours.

Turn one foil over VERY CAREFULLY onto your serving platter. It is extremely fragile. Peel foil off very slowly. If it breaks it is still okay, just overlap the pieces.

Place 1/3 orange cream filling on first cookie, spread it out. Add sliced strawberries and 1/3 of grated chocolate. Repeat with the second cookie. Repeat with the third cookie.

On top layer put the cream filling on first, then the grated chocolate, and top with the largest strawberries you can find.

Refrigerate until serving time, but do not layer it more than 2 to 3 hours ahead of serving time or it will loosen up and the crisp layers will get too soft.

Billy in front of our house at 12746 Kling Street.

ORANGE CREAM FILLING:

1 pint whipping cream

1/2 cup sugar

1 tsp. orange peel

2 Tbsp. dark Jamaican rum
(or substitute 3 Tbsp. of
Grand Marnier for the
orange peel and rum)

Whip cream. Add sugar as it starts to stiffen. Then gradually beat in rum or Grand Marnier until well blended.

Note: If the pastry breaks or crumbles when you remove the foil, you can crumble all of the cookie and layer it in individual crystal sherbert glasses with the orange cream and chocolate.

Garnish the top with large berries. It tastes just as good this way & looks equally pretty.

This is always a huge success! Just beware of making this on a damp day or a humid day as the cookie will get soggy.

Judy and Billy

Coffee Eclairs
with Coffee or Chocolate Frosting

This may look like a difficult recipe, but it is not. I have made these many times, and they never fail to get rave reviews!

Cream-Puff Dough:

1/4 cup butter

1/8 tsp. salt

1/2 cup sifted all-purpose flour

2 large eggs

Filling:

1/2 cup whipping cream

2 Tbsp. confectioners sugar

1/2 tsp. powdered instant coffee

1/4 tsp. vanilla

frosting variations
(see page 218)

Cream-Puff Dough:

Preheat oven to 400°.

In small saucepan, slowly bring 1/2 cup water with the butter and salt to a boil.

Remove from heat. With wooden spoon, beat in flour all at once.

Return to low heat and continue beating until mixture forms ball and leaves side of pan. Remove from heat.

Beat in eggs, one at a time, beating hard after each addition until smooth.

Continue beating until dough is shiny and breaks into strands.

Put cream-puff dough into small pastry bag with round decorating tip, 1/2" in diameter.

On an ungreased cookie sheet, 2" apart, press mixture in 2" strips.

Bake 20 to 25 minutes, or until golden-brown. Let cool completely on wire rack.

Makes 32 eclairs.

Filling:

Beat cream with sugar, coffee and vanilla until stiff. Refrigerate, covered, until ready to use.

Assemble Eclairs:

With a sharp knife, cut a slice from top of each eclair.

Fill each with a teaspoon of filling. Replace tops.

Frost tops with coffee frosting *(see next page)*.

Put chocolate frosting *(see next page)* in a small pastry bag. Use the smallest tip (one used for writing) and make a zigzag effect across the top of each eclair on top of the coffee frosting.

Note: Instead of using a pastry bag, you can put the chocolate frosting in a small sandwich bag. Cut a tiny piece off one corner of the bag and decorate eclairs.

Refrigerate until serving.

Judy

(Coffee Eclairs, continued)

COFFEE FROSTING

2 cups sifted confectioners sugar

2 Tbsp. light corn syrup

1 tsp. vanilla

1 tsp. powdered instant coffee

In top of double boiler, combine all ingredients with 2 Tbsp. water.

Stir over hot, not boiling, water just until frosting becomes smooth and shiny and coats a wooden spoon. Remove from hot water.

If frosting thickens, thin it with a little water. Makes about 1 cup.

CHOCOLATE FROSTING

1 Tbsp. butter

2 Tbsp. sugar

1 square unsweetened chocolate

1/2 tsp. vanilla

In small saucepan, combine butter, sugar, chocolate, and 2 Tbsp. water.

Stir over medium heat, until chocolate melts and mixture is smooth and just starts to boil. Remove from heat.

Add vanilla. Let stand 2 minutes before using. Makes 1/3 cup.

RUGELACH

Recipe is from my dear friend Pearl Malkin

Rugelach is a traditional Eastern European pastry. This recipe is from my dear friend Pearl Malkin. Pearl learned how to make it from her mother, who learned it from her mother. It's an old Polish recipe. Pearl was my father's first girlfriend.

1 cup butter (2 sticks), softened

1/2 lb. cream cheese, room temperature

2 cups all purpose flour

raspberry jam

crushed walnuts

golden raisins

cinnamon sugar

Blend the butter, cream cheese, and flour all together with your hands. Mix well with your fingers till it forms a ball of dough.

Divide it into 4 pieces. Form 4 small balls of dough. Cover with wax paper. Refrigerate overnight.

Preheat oven to 350°. Have ready in separate bowls: crushed walnuts, golden raisins, raspberry jam, and cinnamon sugar.

Roll out each dough ball into a round. Cut into twelve wedges. Spread with jam, then sprinkle generously with sugar all over.

Top with raisins and nuts.

Roll each wedge toward the center like a croissant. Bend corners into crescent shape. Put onto greased cookie sheet or Teflon cookie sheet.

Bake at 350°, about 25 minutes until light brown. (Every oven is different, so check to be sure they are not turning too brown.) Remove from oven and cool on wire racks. Makes about four dozen. These freeze beautifully.

Pearl

COOKIES, CANDY, & NUTS

GRANNY'S DOUBLE COOKIES

Recipe from Mary Ann Greene

1/2 lb. salted butter
1/2 cup granulated sugar
1-1/2 cups flour
1 Tbsp. cream
powdered sugar
raspberry jam

Preheat oven to 350°.

Mix butter and sugar well.

Stir in flour.

Stir in cream -- you may need to add additional cream - make the dough usable!

Roll very thin. Covering rolling pin with wax paper helps.

Cut out with a cookie cutter a little larger than a silver dollar. Bake until light brown.

Sandwich 2 cookies together with jam and sprinkle with powdered sugar.

Note: You can cut a shape out of the "top" cookie so that jam shows through when cookies are assembled. I use an hors d'oeuvres cutter.

Mary Ann

PECAN BUTTER FINGERS

Recipe from Tess Braun

1 cup butter, softened
1/2 cup powdered sugar
2 cups flour
1/2 tsp. salt
2 tsp. vanilla
1 cup chopped pecans

Beat together butter and sugar until creamy and fluffy.

Gradually mix in flour.

Stir in salt, vanilla and pecans.

Using level tablespoons of dough, shape into 2" long fingers.

Place on ungreased cookie sheets.

Bake at 350° for 15 to 20 minutes.

Tess

LEMON BARS

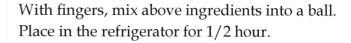

Recipe from Susan Berg

2 cups sifted flour

1 cup butter, softened to room temperature

1/2 cup powdered sugar

4 extra large eggs

2 cups sugar

dash of salt

7 Tbsp. fresh lemon juice

4 Tbsp. flour

1 tsp. baking powder

With fingers, mix above ingredients into a ball. Place in the refrigerator for 1/2 hour.

Butter a 9″ x 13″ cookie sheet that has sides.

Press and pat the dough into the bottom of the cookie sheet, and pierce all over with a fork.

Bake approximately 25 minutes at 350° until light brown all over.

While crust is baking, lightly mix the extra large eggs, sugar, salt, and fresh lemon juice.

Separately mix together 4 Tbsp. flour and baking powder.

Fold flour mixture into the egg mixture. Fold flour mixture into the egg mixture.

After crust has cooked, pour egg mixture over it, and return to oven for approximately 25 minutes, still at 350°.

It's done when slightly brown with craters formed.

Let cool and powder the top with confectioners sugar.

Susan and Judy

MANDEL BREAD

Recipe from Grandma Miriam

4 eggs

2-1/3 cup sugar

1 cup Crisco

4-1/2 Tbsp. cooking oil

1/4 tsp. salt

1/2 cup orange juice

1 Tbsp. vanilla

7 cups of flour mixed with 2 tsp. baking powder

Nut Mixture:

2 tsp. sugar

2 tsp. cinnamon

1 cup chopped walnuts

Blend the eggs, sugar, and Crisco together in KitchenAid mixer at slow speed.

Then add cooking oil, salt, orange juice, vanilla, and 7 cups of flour mixed with 2 tsp. baking powder.

Blend all at slow speed. Separate dough into 4 pieces and refrigerate for one hour. You can bake just one piece and freeze the others until needed.

On a floured board, roll each piece of dough into a long flat strip. Pour nut mixture in middle of each strip or use strawberry jam. Roll up length-wise. Seal dough.

Brush with water. Sprinkle with cinnamon and sugar if filled with nuts. Sprinkle with sugar only if filled with jam.

Place roll on cookie sheet and bake at 350° for 45 minutes. Remove from oven.

Turn up oven to 375°. Slice roll diagonally. Return cookies to baking sheet on their sides. Bake another 20 minutes.

Flip cookies to their other side and bake again until sides are brown.

Grandma Miriam

SPRITZ COOKIES

This recipe came from the wife of one of my father's employee's at Great Western Bag Co., Adolf Cole. They are my daughter Carrie's favorite cookie.

2-1/2 cups flour

1 pinch salt

1/2 tsp. baking powder

1 cup butter or Crisco

1 small Philadelphia cream cheese

3/4 cup sugar

1 egg

1 tsp. vanilla

semi-sweet chocolate chips

Mix flour with salt and baking powder. Set aside.

Combine shortening and cream cheese, add sugar slowly, then add egg and vanilla.

Blend in flour mixture. Using a cookie press, press onto cookie sheet in desired shapes.

Press a few chocolate chips into the dough.

Bake at 400° until brown. About 10 to 15 minutes.

Steven, Carol, and Judy

CHOCOLATE-DIPPED BATONS

1/2 cup butter, room temperature

2/3 cup sugar

2 eggs

1 tsp. vanilla

2-1/2 cups flour

2 tsp. baking powder

4 (1 oz.) squares semi-sweet chocolate

chopped almonds

Cream butter and sugar until light and fluffy. Beat in eggs and vanilla.

Combine flour and baking powder and add to mixture.

Continue beating at low speed until well mixed.

Wrap dough in wax paper and refrigerate at least 2 hours.

Preheat oven to 350°. Divide dough into 8 pieces.

Roll each piece on a lightly floured surface into a 1/2″ wide rope.

Cut into 2″ pieces. Place on greased cookie sheet, 1″ apart.

Bake 10 to 12 minutes until light brown. Cool. Continue with remaining dough.

Melt chocolate in the top of double broiler.

Dip one end of cookie into chocolate, then into chopped almonds.

Cool on wax paper until hard.

Steven and Carol, November 1, 2003

SUGAR COOKIES

Simply the best...ever!

1 cup butter

1 cup sugar

1 cup confectioners sugar

2 eggs

1 cup canola oil

2 tsp. vanilla

4-1/4 cups unsifted flour

1 tsp. baking soda

1 tsp. cream of tartar

1/2 tsp. salt

rainbow-colored sanding sugar

In a large bowl with electric mixer at medium speed, cream butter and sugars.

Beat in eggs one at a time until mixture is light. Add oil and vanilla. Beat until well blended.

In a large bowl, combine flour, baking soda, cream of tartar and salt.

Gradually add dry ingredients to the creamed mixture, and beat until blended.

Wrap dough and chill for several hours.

Roll teaspoonfuls of dough into balls and place on a cookie sheet.

Flatten dough to 2" circles with the bottom of a glass dipped into rainbow colored sanding sugar.

Sprinkle with more sugar if desired.

Bake at 325° for 8 to 10 minutes.

Let stand on the cookie sheet for 2 to 3 minutes before removing. Makes about 7 dozen.

DREAM STREET COOKIES

Recipe from Andrea Bernard

These cookies are great because they are both crunchy and chewy. Great combination!

4 sticks butter, room temperature

2 cups granulated sugar

2 cups brown sugar

4 eggs

2 tsp. vanilla

2 tsp. baking soda

2 tsp. baking powder

2 cups corn flakes

4 cups flour

2 cups oatmeal

1 cup raisins (optional)

12 oz. chocolate chips

Cream together softened butter, sugar, brown sugar and vanilla.

Add the rest of the ingredients.

Bake at 350° until golden brown.

Vanilla Kipfel

Recipe from Tess Braun

1 cup butter

1/2 cup granulated sugar

1/2 tsp. salt

2 cups sifted all purpose flour

2 cups ground almonds (no need to blanch)

1 cup powdered sugar mixed with 1/8 tsp. vanilla bean pulp (or 3/4 cup powdered sugar mixed with 2 packages of vanilla sugar)

Cream together butter, sugar and salt.

Add flour a little at a time, stirring in thoroughly. Add almonds.

Take 1 tsp. of mixture at a time, roll in palm of hand to form crescent.

Lay in rows on a greased cooked sheet and place in HOT oven (400°) to keep the crescents from running.

After 2 minutes reduce heat to 300°.

Bake to a pale yellow, about 10 minutes.

Slightly cool, then roll in powdered sugar mixed with vanilla bean. Yield: 6 dozen crescents.

LADYFINGERS

Recipe from Arlene Grubman

5 egg yolks

1/2 cup plus 1 Tbsp. granulated sugar

1 cup MINUS 1 Tbsp. sifted all purpose flour

3/4 cup egg whites (about 5)

1-1/2 tsp. granulated sugar (to be added to the egg whites)

powdered sugar for dusting

Heat oven to 350°. Beat egg yolks in large mixer bowl on medium speed.

Gradually beat in 1/2 cup plus 1 Tbsp. sugar. Beat until mixture is pale yellow, and falls in smooth stream when dropped from spoon, about 3 minutes. Gently stir in flour.

Beat egg whites in a small mixing bowl until soft peaks form.

Add sugar.

Beat until stiff peaks form.

Gently fold into flour mixture. (Do not over mix. Batter will be lumpy.)

Fit pastry bag with 1/2" plain tip. Spoon mixture into bag.

Pipe batter into 2" long fingers on parchment lined or buttered and floured baking sheets.

Sprinkle with powdered sugar.

Bake until light brown around edges, about 12 minutes.

Cool on wire racks. Makes 4 dozen.

Arlene, Fern, Blanche, and Parke Fiedler

Viennese Almond Sandwich Cookies

I got this recipe from the owner of Aspen's first sushi restaurant.

4-1/2 oz. whole almonds, blanched

1-1/4 cup flour

1/2 cup butter, softened

1/3 cup sugar

1/4 tsp. salt

1/4 cup apricot preserves

Chocolate Glaze:

3 oz. semi-sweet chocolate

1 Tbsp. butter

1 Tbsp. milk

1-1/2 tsp. light corn syrup

Grind almonds. In a large bowl, put flour, butter, sugar and salt. Add almonds.

Knead ingredients until well blended (dough will be very dry). Preheat oven to 350°.

Between 2 sheets of waxed paper, roll 1/2 of the dough to 1/8" thick.

With a 2" cookie cutter, cut out cookies. Place cookies 1/2" apart on ungreased cookie sheet.

Repeat using remaining dough. Bake 8 minutes or until golden.

On one half of the cookies, spread 1/2 tsp. of preserves on bottom of each cookie.

Top with remaining cookies.

Chocolate Glaze:

Melt ingredients over hot, but not boiling, water.

Dip filled cookies edgewise into chocolate mixture to cover half of the cookie sandwich.

Place cookies on waxed paper. Store in fridge. Makes about 2 dozen.

BREAKFAST IN A COOKIE

Sometimes I substitute walnuts for the almonds.

2 cups old-fashioned oats

1-1/4 cups whole wheat flour

1 cup all purpose flour

1 cup Grape-Nuts cereal

1/2 cup wheat germ

1/2 cup oat bran

2 tsp. baking soda

2 cups (4 sticks) unsalted butter, room temperature

2 large eggs

1 cup packed golden brown sugar

1/2 cup granulated sugar

1 Tbsp. vanilla extract

1 cup almonds, about 5 ounces, toasted and coarsely chopped or 1 cup chopped walnuts

1 cup semi-sweet chocolate chips

Preheat oven to 350°.

Blend oats, both flours, Grape-Nuts, wheat germ, oat bran, and baking soda in a large bowl.

Using an electric mixer, beat butter in another large bowl until creamy.

Add eggs, both sugars, and vanilla. Beat until smooth.

Stir in cereal mixture just until blended. Mix in almonds or walnuts, and chocolate chips.

Cover and chill until ready to use, up to one week. The dough can also be frozen at this point. Let soften at room temperature before continuing.

Grease 2 large baking sheets or line with parchment paper. You can also use non-stick baking sheets.

Drop dough in heaping tablespoons onto prepared baking sheets, spacing mounds 2" apart.

Using damp fingers, press cookies to form 1/2" thick rounds.

Bake cookies 1 sheet at a time until brown on top, about 15 minutes.

Let cookies stand on baking sheet 2 to 3 minutes before transferring to rack to cool.

Balsamic Syrup Crisps

Two years ago, I rented a house in Lucca, Italy where the chef prepared these delicious treats. The syrup is great drizzled over pan-roasted chicken too.

1-1/2 cups balsamic vinegar
3 Tbsp. sugar
ciabatta bread, sliced very thin

butter, room temperature

Boil the vinegar and sugar in a small saucepan over medium-high heat until reduced and thick, about 20 minutes.

Stir occasionally. Toast the ciabatta slices in 350° oven for about 5 minutes.

Spread butter on toasts and drizzle with balsamic syrup.

Sprinkle with a little granulated sugar, and serve. When syrup cools, it is even better.

Wes, Marilyn, Andrea and Paul with Chef Bruno and his wife.

CITRUS PECANS

Recipe from Marlene Kamin

3 cups sugar

1 cup water

4 cups whole pecans

1/2 cup grated lemon and orange rind (1/2 cup total)

Combine sugar and water in saucepan. Stir over low heat until sugar dissolves.

Increase heat to medium high and bring to a boil, no stirring, until candy thermometer reaches 240°. Remove from heat.

Stir in pecans and citrus rind. Stir until syrup becomes cloudy.

Turn onto waxed paper and separate clusters into individual nuts before completely hardened. Makes 4 to 5 cups.

May be frozen if you want.

Judy and Marlene

Judy's Sugared Walnuts

3/4 cup sugar

1/4 cup sherry, Grand Marnier
or bourbon

2 cups walnut halves

In a deep saucepan, combine the sugar and liquid and bring to a boil.

Add the walnuts and simmer, stirring, as the water evaporates. The glaze will be shiny and transparent at first, then will turn opaque as the water cooks away.

When the nuts are completely coated with sugar crystals, they are done.

Spread them out on wax paper to cool.

Can be made up to 2 weeks in advance.

Store in airtight container.

(To wash the saucepan, soak it overnight.)

FRESH ROASTED CHESTNUTS

Buy chestnuts that are firm and unblemished.

Preheat oven to 400°.

On the flat side of each chestnut, slit the skin of each nut with an "x" to allow steam to escape as they cook.

Put the nuts on a baking sheet, and bake for 20 to 25 minutes.

When they are cool enough to handle, grasp the curling skin and peel.

CANDY BON BONS

Recipe from Janet DeCarolis

1 quart finely chopped walnuts

1 stick of butter

1-1/2 cups shredded coconut

1 can Eagle Brand
condensed milk

Coating:

1/2 square paraffin wax

12 oz. package semisweet
chocolate chips

Mix walnuts, butter, coconut and condensed milk together. Form into balls. Chill in freezer.

Coating:

Melt wax in top of double boiler.

Add chocolate chips.

Melt until smooth. Dip balls in coating. Place on wax paper.

Cook's note: I use a long toothpick for dipping.

Janet is my daughter-in-law's lovely mother.

DRINKS

ORANGE JULIUS

Recipe is from Steven's and Carrie's father,

Bill Braun

2 cups of orange juice

1/2 cup cream

1/2 cup water

1/4 cup sugar

1/2 tsp. vanilla

5-6 ice cubes

1 pasteurized egg

Mix all of the ingredients in a blender and serve.

Roxbury Park, Beverly Hills

THE MINE CO. RUM PUNCH

3/4 oz. white rum

3/4 oz. dark rum

1-1/2 oz. orange juice

1-1/2 oz. pineapple juice

1-1/2 oz. sweet/sour
(buy at any liquor store)

3 dashes grenadine

Shake.

Pour over ice.

Andrea and Ken Bernard owned The Mine Co.
It was one of Aspen's most popular restaurants.

LIMONCELLO

8 lemons

1 (750 liter) bottle of unflavored vodka

2 cups of water

2 cups of sugar

Peel 8 lemons. Use yellow rind only, as the white part will make it bitter. Put lemon peels in a glass bowl.

Pour vodka over lemon peels. Cover bowl.

Put in a cool, dark cupboard for 7 to 12 days.

Put 2 cups of water in a pot. Add 2 cups of sugar and heat until the sugar is completely dissolved. Let sugar solution cool to room temperature.

Pour lemon and alcohol solution through a strainer into the cool sugar water.

Put in bottle. Put bottle in freezer.

You can use this recipe to make Orange Blossom liqueur. Substitute 1 1/2 cups orange blossoms for the lemon rind.

Sam Fiedler

EGG CREAM

This recipe is from my dad, Seymour Grubman

Billy, Patty, and I agree...he is simply the best father in the world!

2 Tbsp. chocolate syrup
1/4 cup cold milk
4-6 oz. cold seltzer

Pour chocolate syrup into a glass.

Pour milk over syrup and stir.

Add seltzer and stir again.

Seymour and Judy

GINGER TEA

My mother once had a Chinese housekeeper who told us that fresh ginger was an old Chinese remedy for stomach ailments. So...if you've eaten too much of the good food you've prepared...try this.

fresh ginger
water
honey

Steep a few slices of fresh ginger in boiling water.

Add honey to taste.

Arlene

KITCHEN TIPS

MEASURE LIQUIDS in a glass or clear plastic measuring cup with a pouring spout.

MEASURE DRY INGREDIENTS in dry measuring cups that can be leveled off with a knife.

MEASURE FLOUR by spooning into a dry measuring cup that can be leveled off with a knife.

SALT: All salt measurements are for table salt unless otherwise specified.

BLACK PEPPER: Should always be freshly ground.

SPICES: Store in a cool dark place.

WATER BATH FOR BAKING: Put filled pan into a larger pan and place in oven. Then add enough boiling water to the large pan to reach halfway up the side of the smaller pan.

CITRUS ZEST: Remove the colored part of the rind only. Avoid the bitter white pith. Use a vegetable peeler for strips.

TO KEEP PRE-MADE SANDWICHES FRESH: When making a large quantity of sandwiches for a crowd, wrap each sandwich with a moist paper towel, then cover with plastic wrap. This method will keep the sandwich fresh.

FOR SWEETER, BETTER TASTING RAW ONIONS: If you are using raw onions in any recipe, rinse the sliced or chopped onions under running water. Pat dry before using.

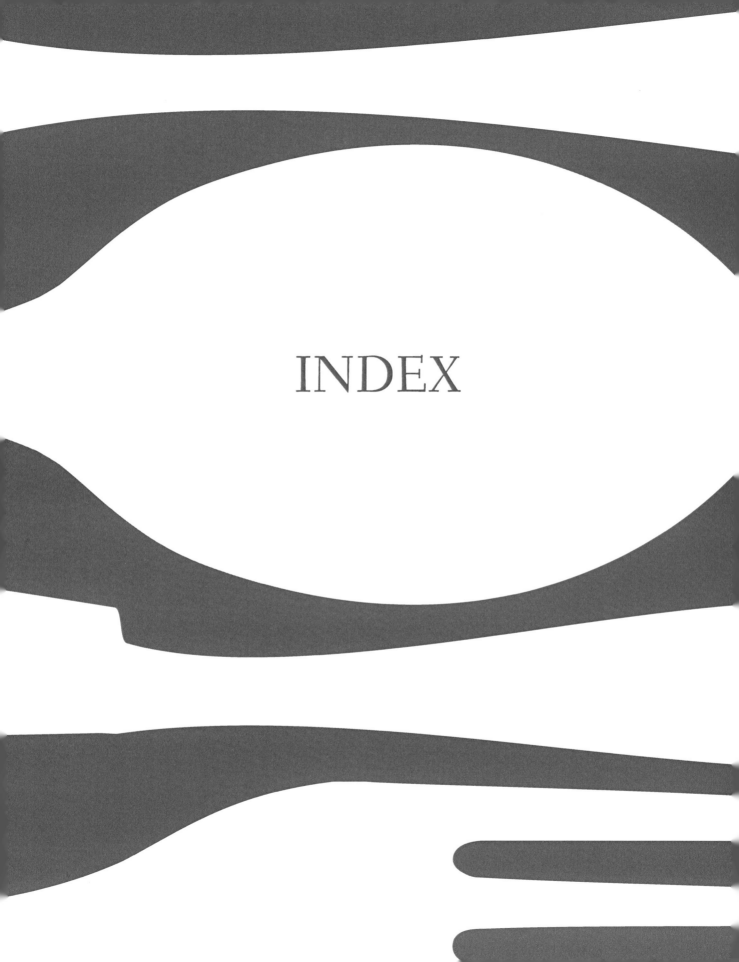

INDEX

A special thank you to Heidi Lopez-Seid

for her help in putting together this book.

*All Proceeds from the Sale of This Book Will Benefit
the Dream Street Foundation*

The Dream Street Foundation, a non-profit corporation founded in 1988, provides camping programs for children with chronic and life threatening illnesses. The usual sleep-away camps are not able to meet the needs of children who require medication daily or several times a day. At Dream Street, our volunteer counselors, as well as our medical staff, are available 24 hours a day to care for the children. Children at Camp Dream Street are given the opportunity to enjoy the experiences normally restricted due to their illness. Over 750 children attend Dream Street's programs each summer. At present, Dream Street funds and operates programs in California, Arkansas, New Jersey, Mississippi and Arizona.

Dream Street's medical team, counselors, and volunteers donate their time and travel, at their own expense, to participate in our program. Even the medications are donated. Camping sessions are free of charge. The children are flown in by Dream Street from around the city, country and sometimes overseas.

Like the camping staff, the Dream Street Foundation and Board of Directors is made up entirely of volunteers. These people create and staff the fund-raising events as well as helping with camp activities. All funds go directly to the camping programs.

Made in the USA
San Bernardino, CA
19 January 2015